The New York Times

EASY CROSSWORD PUZZLES
VOLUME 23

First published in the United States by St. Martin's Griffin,
an imprint of St. Martin's Publishing Group

THE NEW YORK TIMES EASY CROSSWORD PUZZLES VOLUME 23.
Copyright © 2022 by The New York Times Company. All rights reserved.
Printed in China. For information, address St. Martin's Press,
120 Broadway, New York, NY 10271.

www.stmartins.com

All of the puzzles that appear in this work were originally published
in *The New York Times* from August 3, 2020, to July 21, 2021,
by The New York Times Company. All rights reserved.
Reprinted by permission.

ISBN 978-1-250-83177-4

Our books may be purchased in bulk for promotional, educational, or business use.
Please contact your local bookseller or the Macmillan Corporate and Premium Sales Department
at 1-800-221-7945, extension 5442, or by email at MacmillanSpecialMarkets@macmillan.com.

First Edition: 2022

10 9 8 7 6 5 4 3 2 1

The New York Times

EASY CROSSWORD PUZZLES VOLUME 23
50 Monday Puzzles from the Pages of *The New York Times*

Edited by Will Shortz

ST. MARTIN'S GRIFFIN
NEW YORK

Looking for more Easy Crosswords?

The New York Times

The #1 Name in Crosswords

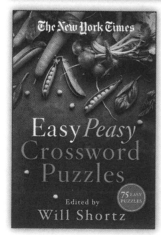

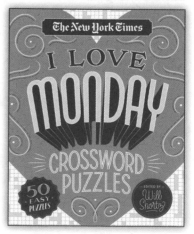

Available at your local bookstore or online at
us.macmillan.com/author/thenewyorktimes

 ST. MARTIN'S GRIFFIN

ACROSS

1 Home of Pago Pago
6 Muscles that get "crunched" in crunches
9 [Oh, well]
13 Things that go off when there's danger
16 Other: Sp.
17 Where to go for a fill-up
18 Mets' venue before Citi Field
19 Regarding
20 ___ San Lucas (Mexican resort city)
21 Member of a tough crowd, say
22 Firm place to plant your feet
24 "That sounds fun to me!"
28 "Auld ___ Syne"
29 Tuesday, in Toulouse
30 Ancient carver of stone heads in Mesoamerica
33 Move on a pogo stick
36 Viewing options popularized in the 1990s
39 ___ card (smartphone insert)
40 Beefcakes
41 Doesn't win
42 H₂O, south of the border
44 "So's your mama!," for one
45 Cash or stock, e.g.
50 Child's counterpart
51 Witty remark
52 "I'll get right ___"
56 Christmas carol
57 The terrible twos, e.g. (one hopes!) . . . or the start of 17-, 22-, 36- or 45-Across?
59 Protected, at sea
60 Floral garland
61 "Money ___ everything"
62 Opposite NNW
63 Halves of quarts

DOWN

1 Long story
2 "What a shame!"
3 What a sail is tied to
4 Approximately
5 Quantity: Abbr.
6 "I was with my girlfriend all evening," e.g.
7 Donation to the Red Cross
8 Info in a data breach: Abbr.
9 "Leaving already?"
10 "That seemed right to me, too"
11 Like most vegetation
12 Keep everything for oneself
14 Breakfast sizzler
15 And others: Abbr.
21 "Charming" jewelry?
22 What a skinny-dipper lacks
23 Kind of club for singers
24 Little rapscallions
25 Home of Timbuktu
26 Theatrical sort
27 Takes too much, in brief
30 Buckeyes' sch.
31 12, for ⅓, ¼ and ⅙: Abbr.
32 "The Marvelous ___ Maisel"
34 On top of
35 Surreptitious sound during an exam
37 Slightly
38 Word repeated in "Waste ___, want ___"
43 Throat
44 Give back to
45 Hawaiian porch
46 "Golden" things in the Bible
47 Light blue shades
48 Actress Essman of "Curb Your Enthusiasm"
49 Takes a chair
52 "Huh, funny running into you!"
53 Indian flatbread
54 "That true?"
55 Bills with Alexander Hamilton on them
57 Attys.' degrees
58 Drug also known as angel dust

by Eric Bornstein

ACROSS

1 Bay of Pigs locale
5 Constricting snakes
9 Actor who's the opposite of subtle
12 "Moby-Dick" captain
13 Large group on the move
14 Drink such as Pepsi
15 Justice's garb
16 Designation on many a driver's license
18 Bashful
19 Holder for coffee or beer
20 Attics
21 Farm building with a loft
23 Giant . . . with four of the five letters of "giant"
24 Bright, sunny area of a house
27 Setting at the prime meridian, for short
30 Pealed
31 "No more seats," in brief
32 Uncritically enthusiastic, colloquially
34 Confess (to)
36 Fruit in Newton cookies
38 Leather for fine gloves
39 Disdainful looks
41 Seoul automaker
43 Kind of ball that's supersoft
44 President after F.D.R.
45 Launch vehicle for many NASA missions
48 Miley who played Hannah Montana
49 ___ scale (rater of mineral hardness)
50 Insects that may emerge after 17 years
53 Play-___ (toy clay)
54 Boat that sailed while it rained for 40 days and nights
57 Ringlet on a salon floor
59 Bit of evidence for Sherlock

60 Author Rice who created the vampire Lestat
61 Pro Football Hall-of-Fame QB John
62 Like pie, it's said
63 "Gangnam Style" musician
64 Salon colorings
65 Dedicated poems

DOWN

1 Autos
2 "This doesn't look good . . ."
3 Wee one's sun protection
4 "Honest" president
5 Tennis champ Björn
6 Dot follower in a nonprofit's web address
7 In slow tempo
8 One of 100 on the Hill
9 Sharpen
10 Oodles
11 Destination of the rover Perseverance
13 Hunting dogs
14 ___ on the cob
17 Serious stage plays
19 Hosp. scan
22 Bicker
23 Groups of three
24 Next year's soph
25 Things to be mowed
26 Doggie's sound
27 Colorful dish with olives and feta cheese
28 Mother: Sp.
29 Larceny
33 Intuitive feeling
35 "Yes, proceed!," quaintly
37 Graduates of basic training, informally

40 Machine-gunned from the air
42 Weapons storehouse
46 In profusion, as plant growth
47 "This is so-o-o amazing!"
48 What you can't have and eat, too, it's said
50 Applaud
51 Charged particles
52 Big Apple school inits.
53 "Buenos ___"
55 Sly stratagem
56 Typically lost items that are "found" in the starts of 16-, 24-, 45- and 57-Across
58 Wonderment
59 Corporate biggie

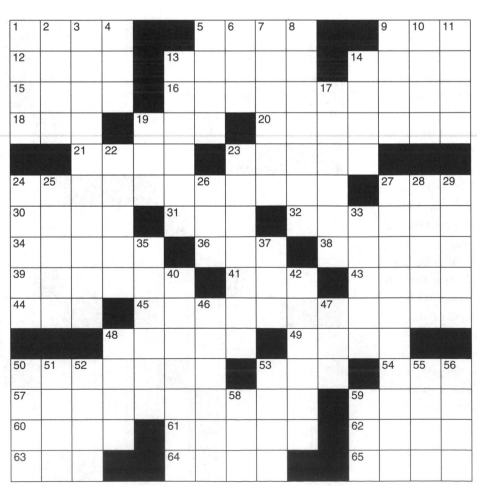

by Lynn Lempel

ACROSS

1 Goes a-courting
5 Buddies
9 Off-the-cuff remark
14 Em, to Dorothy, in "The Wizard of Oz"
15 Openly acknowledge
16 Garlic-flavored mayonnaise
17 "In __ of flowers . . ."
18 Greets from across the way, say
20 Lollygags
22 That is to say, in Latin
23 Casually browse online
26 Word before taught or effacing
30 "Tiny" Dickens boy
31 Drop of golden sun
32 Skin care product
33 Extremes of the earth
35 Time of lament
36 Spends moolah
39 Little VW
40 Displays of huffiness
41 Fruit-filled pastries
42 Illusionist Geller
43 Modern term of endearment
46 __ ID
47 Demonstrates some sleight of hand
51 Should arrive any minute now
53 Ice cream serving
54 Property along the ocean . . . or a hint to the starts of 18-, 23-, 36- and 47-Across
59 Dance at Jewish weddings
60 Hanukkah potato treat
61 Again
62 Shooting star, some might think
63 Lock of hair
64 __ lily
65 Greek peak in Thessaly

DOWN

1 Financial ctr. in Manhattan
2 "Most definitely, monsieur!"
3 Feature of a Las Vegas "bandit"
4 Things, collectively
5 Dog's foot
6 Director DuVernay of "Selma"
7 The __ Spoonful (1960s pop group)
8 Stockholm native
9 Companion of "oohs"
10 Low-calorie drinks
11 Ha-ha, online
12 Sick
13 Info in a Who's Who listing
19 Cry between "Ready" and "Go!"
21 Leisurely walks
24 Actress Berry
25 Centers of hurricanes
27 Extremities
28 Jacob's first wife, in the Bible
29 Cook in oil
32 Elements of a strategy
33 "Stupid" segments on old David Letterman shows
34 "We need help!"
35 Mixes with a spoon, say
36 Caspian and Caribbean
37 Reply in a roll call
38 E pluribus __
39 Air-conditioning meas.
43 Needs for playing Quidditch
44 Is gaga over
45 Madrid's land, to locals
47 File shareable on a PC or Mac
48 Psychic glows
49 Sierra __ (African country)
50 Sound preceding "Gesundheit!"
52 The Beatles' "__ Leaving Home"
54 Sandwich inits.
55 Put a ring on it!
56 Gobbled up
57 Less than zero: Abbr.
58 What it takes to tango

by Alan Massengill and Andrea Carla Michaels

4

ACROSS

1 State of irritability
5 Oaf
9 Undercoat of an oil painting
14 Cabernet, e.g.
15 Opening stake
16 "Oh, no, not __!"
17 Stress between you and your former lover?
19 Carried
20 "In excelsis __"
21 One of a pair of Old Testament books with female names
23 Place for a baseball team's insignia
24 Canada's Prince __ Island
26 Thing your former lover said about you?
29 Straight up on a compass
32 The Beatles' "__ Leaving Home"
33 Historian's concern
36 "QB VII" author Leon
38 Halved
41 Former lover's text, e.g.?
44 What alumni do on important anniversaries
45 Write with a chisel on stone
46 Cold summer treats
47 Something Santa makes (and checks twice)
49 Aptitude
51 Former lovers' stances in photos?
54 Absolutely everything
58 See 27-Down
59 Juneau's home
62 Singer Grande, informally
63 Busy, as a restroom
66 Current lover who seems suspiciously preoccupied?
68 Chef's item for preparing apples
69 Panache
70 Author unknown, for short
71 Arrogant look
72 Things janitors keep on rings
73 Wagers

DOWN

1 Neighbor of a Norwegian
2 Vetoed
3 Dragging behind
4 Prop for a golf ball
5 Percussion instrument in a marching band
6 Hop __ (get to work)
7 Texter's transition
8 Actress Zellweger
9 Gift of __
10 Latin "I"
11 Like "Yeah, that'll ever happen"
12 Mideast's __ Peninsula
13 End of a lunch hour, maybe
18 Emperor just before the Year of the Four Emperors
22 Prescriptions, for short
25 Villain in Shakespeare's "The Tempest"
27 With 58-Across, 1980s fad that "sprouted"
28 Soup legumes
30 Factual
31 Clues
33 The "p" of b.p.s.
34 It can chop a tree down . . . and then chop a tree up
35 Three-dimensional art
37 Ailing
39 Tale of __
40 Come-__ (enticements)
42 Target of a cleanup
43 Fraidy-cats
48 Throat soother
50 Money to tide you over
51 Long stories
52 Arc lamp gas
53 Aerodynamic
55 Augusta's home
56 "Believe It __!"
57 Yield and Right Turn Only, e.g.
60 Connector of a pair of wheels
61 Fix, as a dog
64 "Get it?"
65 Go wrong
67 Smidgen

by David Alfred Bywaters

ACROSS

1 Criticize, in slang
4 Something computers cannot write to or erase
9 Bottomless pit
14 "We ___ the World"
15 Nice smell
16 Like some handwriting . . . or tipplers
17 Up to, informally
18 Traveled in the front passenger seat
20 ___ at the wheel
22 Lye, chemically
23 Rainbow's shape
24 "Heavens to ___!"
26 Two-part
28 Captain of the 2012 and 2016 U.S. women's Olympic gymnastics teams
31 Degs. for C.E.O.'s
35 Chap
36 Pants part that might need patching
37 Join a conference call, say
39 Silly
41 Monopoly properties you can't put houses on, in brief
43 End of a lasso
44 Screen ___ Guild
46 Rating between excellent and fair
48 Cry in a soccer stadium
49 Watermelon part that's spit out
50 Main ingredient in a protein shake, maybe
53 Great Lake with the shortest name
55 Mommy's sister
56 Kind of connection port on a PC
59 Overly fussy, say
61 Hit Broadway musical set partly in Paris, for short
64 What you might do to pass on an interstate . . . or a phonetic hint to the starts of 18-, 28- and 50-Across

67 Letters before an assumed name
68 Sudden forward thrust
69 "___ could've told you that!"
70 ___ center
71 Choice words?
72 Believer in Jah, informally
73 Pack animal of the Himalaya

DOWN

1 Facts and figures
2 Part of the eye
3 Stamp on a milk carton
4 One tending a house during the owner's absence
5 Stops by
6 Towel holder
7 Eclipse or a black cat, some say
8 Ancient fortification overlooking the Dead Sea
9 Hi in HI
10 Spam spewer
11 Some quiet exercise
12 Appendage on a cowboy's boot
13 Align, informally
19 Elvis's "___ Dog"
21 Always, to a poet
25 Belgian river to the North Sea
27 "Hilarious!," in a text
28 Assumed name
29 Knight's weapon
30 Join the flow of traffic
32 Cocktail with tomato juice
33 Seating request on an airplane
34 Mocking smile
38 World's largest island nation
40 Lymph ___

42 Tofu bean
45 Hogs
47 Luxurious
51 Doctor, ideally
52 Lbs. and ozs.
54 Wild party, in slang
56 Sch. whose home football games used to include a live bear on the field
57 Avoid
58 Extracurricular activity for a musician
60 Molten flow
62 International furniture chain
63 "The Suite Life of ___ & Cody" (bygone teen sitcom)
65 Amnesty International, e.g., in brief
66 Super ___ (1990s game console)

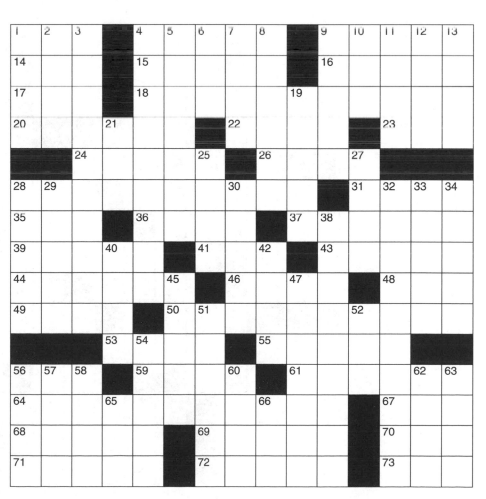

by Anne Marie Crinnion

ACROSS

1 Something that may be bitten or busted
4 No laughing ___
10 "___-voom!"
14 DuVernay who directed "Selma"
15 Printing goofs
16 "___ go bragh!"
17 Entranceway to London's Hyde Park
19 Brainy sort
20 Starting stake
21 Summer coolers, for short
22 Eye makeup
23 "Yee-___!"
25 Kids' game that usually ends in a draw
28 Eternal
31 Ranter's emotion
32 "No lie!"
33 Designer Oscar ___ Renta
34 Go "boo-hoo-hoo!"
37 Singer Yoko
38 North Carolinian
40 Safe Drinking Water Act enforcer, for short
41 Japanese moolah
42 Actress Jessica
43 Speaks impertinently to
45 Classic pie crust ingredient
46 "The birds and the bees"
47 Popular food fish that's actually a flounder
51 Thanksgiving side dish
52 How the surprised are taken
53 Miracle on ___ (1980 Winter Olympics upset)
55 Greek cheese
58 Ending for "right to" or "put to"
59 How tall Barbie is . . . or what the ends of 17-, 25-, 38- and 47-Across are?
62 Connecting point
63 Joseph who wrote "Heart of Darkness"
64 Roth ___ (investment)
65 "S.N.L." bit
66 Artists' stands
67 What prevents a coffee cup from spilling

DOWN

1 "Rama ___ Ding Dong" (1961 hit)
2 Any of several Russian czars
3 Temple on Athens's Acropolis
4 Blanc who voiced Bugs Bunny, Daffy Duck and Porky Pig
5 Geometry calculation
6 Political or religious pamphlets
7 Some ankle bones
8 And so on: Abbr.
9 When repeated, very enthused
10 Home to St. Mark's Basilica
11 "There ___ enough hours in the day . . ."
12 "Black-capped" or "yellow-throated" songbird
13 ___ the Giant (legendary 7'4" wrestler)
18 "If ___ Street Could Talk," 2018 film for which Regina King won an Oscar
22 California soccer club
24 Where Jericho and Bethlehem are located
26 First Nations tribe
27 Author Gay
28 "___, matey!"
29 Disappeared
30 Alternative to an elevator
33 UPS alternative
34 Staple of Asian cooking
35 German auto
36 Sunbathe
39 Start over
44 Aides, collectively
45 Old-fashioned keepsake
46 Like passwords, one hopes
47 Playing surfaces for croquet
48 Some downloadable reading
49 Tuesday, in Tours
50 Civic club whose motto is "We Serve"
54 And others: Abbr.
56 Singer Amos
57 Slightly
59 King beater
60 Pet with which you might form a tight bond
61 Drawbacks to a free app

by Gareth Bain

ACROSS

1 Insect that builds a paper nest
5 Takes a breather
10 Fig. of total economic output
13 Mayberry boy of 1960s TV
14 Make legal
15 Logs, for a fire
16 Riddled (with)
17 Lamented Princess of Wales
18 Sin often associated with green
19 Major-league team from the Motor City
22 Frozen H_2O
23 Female deer
24 Not quite right
27 Start of a tennis rally
29 "Hold your horses!"
32 Variety
34 Prefix often associated with green
35 "You there!"
36 Ballot for candidates of more than one party
40 One that gives a hoot?
42 Humor
43 Container at a beer bash
44 Number of minutes on hold before getting a customer representative
47 Greek I's
51 Two-___ sword
52 Precollege exam
54 Genetic material
55 Comes out ahead in either case . . . as exemplified by 19-, 29-, 36- and 44-Across?
60 Sources of much spam
62 Helper in conning
63 Nuptial exchange
64 At no cost
65 Stage before metamorphosis
66 Gambling mecca north of Carson City
67 Gave a meal to
68 Helpers
69 Genesis garden

DOWN

1 "People are saying . . ."
2 Each
3 Kitchen gizmo for flour
4 Equal
5 SiriusXM medium
6 Best of the best
7 Part of a window blind
8 Morrison who wrote "Beloved"
9 Gala giveaways
10 Item with cross hairs
11 Home of Carson City: Abbr.
12 Two-___ toilet paper
15 Physicist Enrico after whom element #100 is named
20 Three-time Pro Bowler ___ Beckham Jr.
21 Dine
25 "Nevertheless, ___ persisted"
26 Porker's quarters
28 Big shot, for short
29 Italian for "seven"
30 French for "here"
31 Tick-___
33 Green-fleshed fruit
36 How a person might feel after being passed over for a promotion
37 "Tiny" Dickens boy
38 Singer Urban
39 A narcissist has a big one
40 Be in debt
41 Lump of chewing gum
45 What good movie trailers do
46 Gridiron scores, for short
48 Sent to another team
49 "Can I get a volunteer? Somebody . . . ?"
50 Jeans brand popular in the 1980s
52 Do, as a crossword
53 Book of maps
56 Mallorca, e.g.
57 Bangkok native
58 Something "in the hand" that's "worth two in the bush"
59 Something an informant might wear
60 Very close pal, informally
61 Mine cart contents

by John Guzzetta

ACROSS

1 Musical pieces for one instrument
6 Enthusiastic
10 Shoot out
14 Literary heroine who cries "Curiouser and curiouser!"
15 Apex predator of the ocean
16 Bear whose bed is too soft, in a children's story
17 Time to watch boxing on TV
19 Vases
20 To the greatest extent
21 "Hmm, I'm intrigued . . ."
23 .
24 Like getting a $2 bill in change
25 Gulped
28 Modern request to attend
30 One rushing in to save the day
33 Mess up
37 "___ your price!"
38 One of the housewives on "Desperate Housewives"
39 Tears out of the ground
41 Ingratiates
43 Noggin
44 ___ at hand
46 It's on the plus side
47 It makes your pupils constrict
50 Hawaiian kind of porch
51 Floral wreath
52 Stay in touch?
56 Venusians and Martians, in brief
57 Motion accompanying the words "There, there"
60 Martial art with a belt system
62 Carry
64 "Precisely!"
67 Greek counterpart of Cupid
68 Citrus fruit that won't win any beauty contests?

69 First-stringers
70 Snakes spawned by Medusa's blood, in Greek myth
71 Requests
72 Carried

DOWN

1 Less risky
2 Tony who played for 15 seasons with the Minnesota Twins
3 Large hybrid cat
4 Brownish-yellow
5 Goes down, as the sun on the horizon
6 Kind of pond in a Japanese garden
7 Small work unit
8 Sound in a long, empty hallway
9 Alliance HQ'd in Brussels
10 Bird in Liberty Mutual ads

11 Annual New Orleans celebration
12 Paradoxical response to a door knock
13 Pepsi Challenge, for one
18 Witness to the first rainbow in the Bible
22 Rooster's mate
26 Glittery addition to a Christmas tree
27 Info on an airport monitor, for short
29 Emanations to be picked up
30 Repeated question from an owl?
31 Come out
32 When doubled, a popular number puzzle
33 Foamy drink made with tapioca
34 Ones "standing by" in an infomercial

35 Railroad station
36 Cuban line dance
40 Explosive stuff
42 Slangy pronoun
45 Be sick
48 Au courant
49 Walk in the woods
52 ___-Lay (corn chip maker)
53 Enthusiastic
54 ___ Hunt, role for Tom Cruise in "Mission: Impossible"
55 "I've got this"
58 Water color
59 Harbor boats
61 Horse developed in the desert
63 Curve in the road
65 Kind
66 "My country, ___ of thee . . ."

by Daniel Larsen and the Wave Learning Festival Crossword Class

ACROSS

1 "Aida" composer
6 "Do it now!"
10 "Play It as It Lays" author Didion
14 Embellish
15 Note to a staffer
16 "___ us a son is given"
17 Celebrations with hula dancing
18 Support the pasture entrance?
20 Calorie-counting regimen
22 Patron
23 Movies, informally
24 Check someone's parent to make sure she's of drinking age?
27 Pong game company
29 ___ loss for words
30 Russian space station until 2001
31 Liza Minnelli musical set in Berlin
33 Peaty places
35 Church official
37 Was introduced to the doctor?
42 Swirling currents
43 Lift on a ski slope
45 Small, lobsterlike crustacean
48 "Life Is Good" rapper
51 Thurman on the big screen
52 Derby entrant
53 Do some trawling at sea?
55 Gobbled up or down
56 Capital of Latvia
59 Sort
60 Criticize Sega's hedgehog design?
63 Annoying summer swarms
66 And all the rest, in brief
67 Actress Reid of the "American Pie" films
68 Not important
69 "___ we forget"
70 Truant G.I.'s infraction
71 Big health insurer

DOWN

1 Kilmer who played Batman
2 End of a college web address
3 Driver's furious fit
4 Priestly Gaul or Celt
5 Pants line that's partly hidden
6 Loudening device, informally
7 Blood fluid
8 "Famous" cookie guy
9 Head of the Holy See
10 Container for cider or ale
11 Equal in rank
12 Apparel
13 Dead end sign
19 Language of the Quran
21 "That's personal stuff I didn't need to hear"
24 Taxi
25 Itsy-bitsy bit
26 Corsage flower
28 Not stated directly
31 Brand of small planes
32 Radio journalist Shapiro
34 Frets (over)
36 Corrosive cleaner
38 Venomous vipers
39 Smartphone precursor, for short
40 Plentiful
41 Partner of rank and serial number
44 Dirty rotten scoundrel
45 Small place of worship
46 Turn on an axis
47 Large sports venues
49 "Don't ___!"
50 Scarlet letter, e.g.
53 Capital near the only one of the Seven Wonders of the Ancient World that's still largely intact
54 Redheaded orphan of Broadway
57 Smidgen
58 Bite like a beaver
61 Computer key not pressed alone
62 Ripken who played a record 2,632 consecutive major-league games
64 2,000 pounds
65 Mexican Mrs.: Abbr

by Lynn Lempel

ACROSS

1 Access code to use an A.T.M.
4 Inventor's goal
10 Banking org. founded during the Great Depression
14 Opposite of WNW
15 Dickens's "___ Twist"
16 Actress Garr of "Tootsie"
17 Unedited film
19 Degs. for entrepreneurs
20 Marie Curie's research partner and husband
21 In accordance with
23 Dress in India
24 East Coast rival of Caltech
26 Sam who directed the "Evil Dead" series
29 Off-the-wall concepts
33 Worker for a feudal lord
34 In a sorry state
35 Director Lee
38 "Gross! Nobody wants to hear that!"
39 ___ Majesty the Queen
40 One-named singer with the 2014 hit "Chandelier"
41 Beer brand whose popularity didn't drop during the 2020 pandemic, surprisingly
43 "Dead ___ Society"
45 Committed accounting fraud
49 Bind tightly
50 Newsroom figs.
51 Equipment in Monopoly and Yahtzee
53 Like Galileo, by birth
55 Make calm
57 Uptight sort
59 Shade of brown
62 "East of ___" (Steinbeck novel)
63 Supreme Court justice Stephen
64 Friend in France
65 "No thanks"
66 Extends, as a subscription
67 "Golly!"

DOWN

1 People in police "walks"
2 Book after Song of Solomon
3 What a revolution may usher in
4 Rich's opposite
5 ___ vera
6 Relative of a chickadee
7 "Little" girl in "Uncle Tom's Cabin"
8 Nullify
9 Number between dos and cuatro
10 Md. home to the U.S. Cyber Command
11 Gets intel from after a mission
12 $$$ put away for old age
13 Opposite of trans, in gender studies
18 Bit of embellishment
22 Before
24 Travelers to Bethlehem, in Matthew
25 "I Like ___" (1950s political slogan)
27 Hawaii surfing destination
28 Majorca, e.g.: Sp.
30 Kind of center with exercise machines
31 "Fine, stay angry!"
32 Nerd
35 No. on a bank statement
36 Koh-i-___ diamond
37 Band hangers-on
39 Tools for tilling
42 Gestures of approval
43 Goal after a master's, for short
44 Gomorrah's sister city
46 Professor's goal
47 Army knapsack
48 Devious plot
52 Spooky
54 Dict. tag
55 Dish from a crockpot
56 Not mine alone
57 Vim
58 Nutrition fig.
60 Kylo ___, Jedi-in-training seduced to the dark side
61 Bill, the Science Guy

by Evan Mahnken

ACROSS

1 Winning a blue ribbon
5 San ___ (California city, informally)
9 Trite
14 State as fact
15 Toy that hurts when you step on it barefoot
16 Defendant's excuse
17 Some deep voices
19 Kind of snack chip
20 Letter container: Abbr.
21 Have debts
22 When a plane is due to leave, for short
24 Sweetie
25 Her: Fr.
27 Parts of gas stoves
29 Like movies with considerable sex or violence
31 "___ a stinker?" (Bugs Bunny catchphrase)
32 Friendship
33 Kind of cherry
34 Electrical adapter letters
38 "Dee-lish!"
39 Mash-up
42 Paris street
43 One who's well-versed in the arts?
45 Stout and porter
46 Protein builder, informally
48 Sharp or sour in taste
50 Fireplace log holders
51 Where touchdowns are scored
54 Prefix with business or culture
55 Seoul-based automaker
56 Pretty ___ picture
57 "Dude"
58 College in Cedar Rapids, Iowa
61 They were released from Pandora's box
63 "That was fortunate"
66 Special Forces headgear
67 One of several on a superhighway
68 Analogy phrase
69 "Get Yer ___ Out!" (Rolling Stones live album)
70 School founded by Henry VI
71 Auto license issuers, for short

DOWN

1 Sweetie
2 Actress ___ Rachel Wood
3 Be in jail
4 Prefix with cycle
5 With 50-Down, place that this puzzle grid represents
6 Descartes who said "I think, therefore I am"
7 Grow older
8 Some facial jewelry
9 One holding people up
10 Pie ___ mode
11 Limited kind of market
12 Despise
13 Detroit pro team
18 "See? What'd I say!"
23 Polynesian kingdom
26 Tennis do-over
27 Brand of Irish cream liqueur
28 ___ Fáil (ancient crowning stone)
29 Skatepark feature
30 Bullets and such
33 United States symbol
35 "You did it all wrong!," e.g.
36 Hill on a beach
37 Corp. V.I.P.'s
40 Important pipes
41 Actress Robbie of "I, Tonya"
44 Cartoon "devil," informally
47 Damage in appearance
49 The U.S. has East and West ones
50 See 5-Down
51 Barely make it
52 Skin care brand since 1911
53 Milk and cheese products, collectively
57 Lead singer for U2
59 Airing
60 Self-identities
62 Meadow
64 Feedbag tidbit
65 Placed so as not to be found

by Joe Hansen

ACROSS

1 President George or George W.
5 Egypt's capital
10 "Casablanca" pianist
13 Start the poker pot
14 Catkin-producing tree
15 What an oenologist is an expert on
16 Anger, in the comics
18 ___ and crafts
19 Broadcast time
20 Ill-tempered
22 Harper who wrote "To Kill a Mockingbird"
23 Scores in baseball
25 Bit of sunshine
26 Refrain syllables in "Deck the Halls"
27 Burden too heavily
32 Honda model with a palindromic name
35 Uttered
36 Just sitting around
37 Letter after phi, chi and psi
38 Channel for Erin Burnett and Don Lemon
39 Make catty remarks from the side
40 Trig, calc, etc.
41 Lose color
42 Voice above baritone
43 Love, jealousy and anger
45 Classic distress call
46 Setting for TV's "Cheers"
47 German car once owned by General Motors
49 Intervening space
52 Peas and peanuts, for two
56 Perfect example
58 Presidential office shape
59 Nervousness, in the comics

61 Arm or leg
62 Country singer Steve
63 Norway's capital
64 Ginger ___
65 White-plumed wader
66 Many souvenir shirts

DOWN

1 ___ metabolism (energy expended at rest)
2 Remove a knot from
3 Mall unit
4 Group of buffalo
5 Prickly plant
6 Basketball great Iverson
7 Wedding words
8 Extend one's tour of duty
9 Arranged alphabetically, e.g.

10 In answer to the request "Talk dirty to me," she sometimes says "The carpet needs vacuuming"
11 Pantry-raiding bugs
12 See-through material
15 Odor, in the comics
17 Percussion instrument made from a gourd
21 Droopy part of a basset hound
24 No-goodnik
26 Idea, in the comics
28 Trellis-climbing plant
29 Chief Norse god
30 Big name in dog food
31 Cousin of an elk
32 Easy ___, easy go
33 Mosque leader
34 Presidential bill-killer

35 Read the U.P.C. of
39 Calm and impassive
41 Observe through a crystal ball, say
44 "Take me as ___"
45 Group of seven
48 Portrait painter Rembrandt ___
49 Bird in a gaggle
50 Enough
51 Money in Mexico
52 Name spelled out in a Kinks hit
53 Like Satan
54 Minecraft or Fortnite
55 Pirate's plunder
57 Gait slower than a gallop
60 Blunder

by Fred Piscop

ACROSS

1 "That ___ a close one!"
4 "Fingers crossed!"
9 Numbers for sports analysts
14 Everyone
15 A physicist or a fashion designer might work with one
16 Hall-of-Famer Banks a.k.a. "Mr. Cub"
17 ___ sauce (sushi condiment)
18 One reading secret messages
20 Edible casing in a stir-fry
22 Singer Carly ___ Jepsen
23 Narrow cut
24 Vends
26 Goddess who lent her name to the capital of Greece
28 Professional joke teller
32 Half-___ (java order)
33 Karl who co-wrote a manifesto
34 Home that may be made of logs
38 Pleasant smell
41 Collectible animation frame
42 Swiss Army ___
43 Point of connection
44 Revise, as text
46 Org. that might ask you to remove your shoes
47 Health professional who has your back?
51 Quick races
54 Title woman in songs by the Beatles and the Spinners
55 Brainstorming output
56 ___ Vegas
59 "Amen to that!"
62 Apt command to an 18-, 28- or 47-Across
65 Actress Mendes
66 Hilo hello
67 Home made of hides
68 1980s gaming console, in brief
69 Mortise's counterpart
70 Department store that once had a noted catalog
71 Like deserts and some humor

DOWN

1 The "murder hornet" is one
2 ___ vera (cream ingredient)
3 Quite cunning
4 "Brrr!"
5 Ruffian
6 Peculiar
7 Person equal to you
8 Idris of TV's "Luther"
9 "Believe me now?"
10 Item rolled to the curb for a pickup
11 Joint below the knee
12 Cross-promotion
13 Sealy competitor
19 500 sheets of paper
21 Farm enclosure
25 Orthodontic device
27 Target of a camper's scalp-to-toe inspection
28 Digitize, in a way
29 Set to zero, as a scale
30 Words to live by
31 Yellow flowers in the primrose family
35 Conclusion a die-hard might stay for
36 "Should that be the case . . ."
37 Close by
39 Hombre-to-be, perhaps
40 Tennis great Arthur
45 Fitness coach
48 Gran Canaria or Mallorca, por ejemplo
49 Wise sayings
50 Nicotine source, informally
51 Try to unearth
52 One-named singer of 2011's "Someone Like You"
53 New Jersey's ___ Hall University
57 Headings in a playbill
58 ___-Ball
60 Penultimate word in many fairy tales
61 "No sweat!"
63 Went on, as errands
64 Hoppy beer choice, briefly

by Eric Bornstein

14

ACROSS

1 Hacky ___ (game)
5 Loud, mocking call
9 Wash with vigor
14 Sound of a chuckle
15 Stare at, as a creep might
16 Principle to fight for
17 Z ___ zebra
18 Poetic foot with a short and a long syllable
19 Opposite of rural
20 Popular dog crossbreed
23 Common dog command
24 Coins in India
27 Have an invisible footprint
32 Whimper
35 ___ and tonic
36 Part of a test that may produce a hand cramp
37 Thurman of "Pulp Fiction"
38 Was gentle with
41 Before, in a poem
42 Tinker Bell, for one
44 Locale of the anvil and the stirrup
45 Vehicle that travels in only one direction
46 One version of poker
50 Actor Nielsen of "Airplane!"
51 Pants might burst at them
55 "S.N.L." offering
59 Commuting option
62 Grand achievement
63 Root used in making poi
64 "Party on, ___!" "Party on, Garth!"
65 Jane Austen novel
66 Lake that feeds into Lake Ontario
67 Newspaper opinion pieces
68 Optimistic
69 Ballpoint points

DOWN

1 Retrieves, as baseballs
2 "The Fox and the Grapes" author
3 Country along Argentina's entire western border
4 Model and reality star Jenner
5 Connect
6 "Holy moly!"
7 Furry red monster of children's TV
8 Having a new life
9 Made a bust?
10 Occupations
11 Massage
12 John Cougar Mellencamp's "R.O.C.K. in the ___"
13 "Big" name in London
21 Barely scrape (by)
22 Batman and Robin are a "dynamic" one
25 Artist's stand
26 Panic
28 Prior to now
29 YouTube clip, informally
30 Ceased
31 Green-___ monster
32 Botch, as a catch
33 Inbox accumulation
34 Relinquish, as one's rights
38 Tornadoes
39 "Wee" fella
40 Botch something
43 Take back, as an offer
45 Add sugar to
47 Skill of an archer
48 Marijuana cigarette, in old slang
49 Use a sentence with a "?"
52 Maker of Asteroids
53 Intermittently available fast-food sandwich
54 High heels, e.g.
56 Version that's just for show
57 Some Thanksgiving side dishes
58 Common dog command
59 Start of every ZIP code in Virginia
60 Genre for Megan Thee Stallion
61 Sailor's "yes"

by Luke Vaughn

ACROSS

1 Thing with pads and claws
4 Wanders
9 Rod, reel, tackle box, etc., for a fisher
13 Olympic Dream Team inits.
14 Place in a mausoleum
16 ___ Tokarczuk, 2018 Literature Nobelist
17 Raiser of the dead?
19 Musk who founded SpaceX
20 Brainstorms
21 Go by, as time
23 Young Scottish lady
24 Financial aid for college that doesn't need to be repaid
27 Country whose name becomes another country if you change the last letter to a Q
29 Person with a basket or cart
31 Mixed-breed dog that's part spaniel
35 "Keen!"
36 "That's ___ from me" (refusal)
37 Arthropod that can roll into a ball
40 Melted chocolate, e.g.
41 Word before mall or poker
43 Right to cross someone else's land
45 Unlucky
48 Start of a newspaper article, in journalese
49 Busy person just before an election
51 Pledge drive giveaway
55 Fix, as a shoe
56 Insects that love wool
57 Appropriate initials of "stuff we all get"
59 Lures for magazine readers
62 Tiny bit
63 Minneapolis's twin city
64 Defining period
65 Banana leftover
66 Cosmetician Lauder
67 Singer Lana Del ___

DOWN

1 Necessity for a teacher
2 Carne ___ (grilled beef dish)
3 Home of Cardiff and Swansea
4 Yanks' foes
5 Number said just before "Liftoff!"
6 ___ snail's pace
7 Edible mushroom with a honeycomb cap
8 Gets a whiff of
9 Flips out
10 Best Actress nominee for "Juno"
11 "A long time ___ in a galaxy far, far away . . ." ("Star Wars" intro)
12 Tried to get elected
15 "Erin go ___!"
18 Elective eye surgery
22 Having tines
24 Big ___, nickname of baseball's David Ortiz
25 Unstable chemical compound
26 Grand ___ National Park
28 Comes down a mountain, in a way
30 Rummage (around)
31 Alternative to Venmo
32 Like some beer at a bar
33 Related to big business
34 Cry to a toreador
38 Hay unit
39 For whom a product designer designs
42 Against the law
44 Trending hashtag beginning in 2017
46 Dots on a transit map
47 What lieutenants do to captains
50 "Trees" in underwater forests
52 It's said to have the thickest fur of any mammal
53 When repeated, comforting words
54 Op-ed piece, e.g.
56 Farm animal that kicks
57 Sample a soda, say
58 Tribulation
60 Back muscle, for short
61 "What?," in Oaxaca

by Kate Hawkins

ACROSS

1 Tricked by doing something unexpectedly, with "out"
6 Original airer of "Doctor Who" and "Monty Python's Flying Circus"
9 Jitter-free jitter juice
14 Slicker, as winter highways
15 Writer Tolstoy
16 Speechify
17 Sweet item at a bakery
19 One streaming on Twitch, maybe
20 Wedding vow
21 "In memoriam" piece
22 Drinking mug
23 Keep watch while a homeowner's away
26 Drs.' co-workers
27 Categorize
30 Zippo
32 Not an original, informally
33 Bar-to-bar activity
37 Skater Lipinski
38 Heart chambers
39 What a smiley or frowny emoji indicates
41 What a speaker or musician may adjust before starting
43 Immature bug
44 Tidy
45 Wagered
46 Green item proffered by Sam-I-Am
48 Easy win
52 Tally mark
54 The "E" in PG&E: Abbr.
55 "___ unto them that call evil good, and good evil": Isaiah
58 In flames
59 Small advances . . . or the progression suggested by the ends of 17-, 23-, 33-, 41- and 48-Across
62 Police trainee
63 Convenience for withdrawing $$$
64 Appear out of nowhere
65 Maples and myrtles
66 Mattress's place
67 Nervous about what's ahead

DOWN

1 Island group whose name is a brand of water
2 Got an A on
3 Metric weight, informally
4 Slithery fish
5 Thirsty
6 Ill-defined shapes
7 Misrepresent
8 Fillies' counterparts
9 Sirius . . . or Lassie, for example?
10 It was: Lat.
11 Job for a cinematographer
12 Didn't go out to a restaurant
13 Some greenery on forest floors
18 Give a drubbing
23 Roman poet who wrote "Seize the day, put no trust in the morrow!"
24 Spanish gold
25 Member of an early Andean civilization
27 Field of Frida Kahlo or El Greco
28 Coal deposit
29 Shore phenomenon around the time of the new and full moons
31 Tablecloth fabric
33 School fund-raising org.
34 "Ode on a Grecian ___"
35 Action on eBay
36 Score before 15, in tennis
38 Lead-in to girl or boy
40 Family man
42 Scented bags
43 Rap's ___ Wayne
45 R-rated, say
46 Put into law
47 Succeed in life
49 Shish ___
50 Gladden
51 Popular health info source
53 First Nations group
55 Shed tears
56 Magnum ___
57 Catch sight of
60 Place to get a mani-pedi
61 Truckload unit

by Jennifer Nutt

ACROSS

1 Talon
5 Sign of a wound's healing
9 Wallace of Fox News
14 Smog, e.g.
15 "This is terrible!"
16 White gemstone
17 White gemstone
18 Australian wind instrument
20 "Hmm, good enough"
22 Way over there, quaintly
23 Minor fender damage
24 Fish eggs
25 Caller of balls and strikes
27 Kind of pudding
29 Hole-digging tool
31 U.S. president who was once president of the Harvard Law Review
33 Fleming who created 007
34 Third-largest city in Japan
36 Rubber gaskets
38 System of underwater mountains
41 Dine at a restaurant
42 Artist's stand
43 Two auto-racing Unsers
44 Exchange
46 City between Phoenix and Mesa
50 Horror film villain with a knife
52 Reggae relative
54 Atmosphere
55 Fraternity party costume made from a bedsheet
56 Forlorn
58 Belfast's province
60 Wedding attendant
63 Book after II Chronicles
64 Like the smell of burning rubber
65 ___-European languages
66 Threadbare
67 Sch. in New Haven, Conn.
68 Insolent talk
69 Place to store garden tools

DOWN

1 Church groups in robes
2 Take-it-with-you computer
3 Pink-flowering shrub
4 In good health
5 Wicked city in Genesis
6 Ho ___ Minh City
7 Tennis's Murray or Roddick
8 Capital of Colombia
9 Lifesaving subj. taught by the Red Cross
10 Longtime "Project Runway" host Klum
11 Communicating by wireless
12 Severe place of confinement
13 "Think" for IBM and "Think outside the bun" for Taco Bell
19 Fills with love
21 Exactly below, on a map
26 Jab
28 ___ lobe (part of the brain)
30 "Dumb" bird
32 Sounded like sheep
35 Tyne Daly or Keira Knightley
37 Not busy
38 Spanish resort island, to locals
39 Delivery room announcement
40 Scottish refusals
41 Locale of Oakland and Alameda
45 One of the Three Musketeers
47 Unleavened bread for Passover
48 Justin Trudeau's father
49 Quick trip to a store and back, e.g.
51 "Sexy ___" (Beatles song)
53 Words of praise
57 Comic Carvey once of "S.N.L."
59 Stitches
61 End of a school's email address
62 Two forms of them are found in 18-, 38- and 60-Across

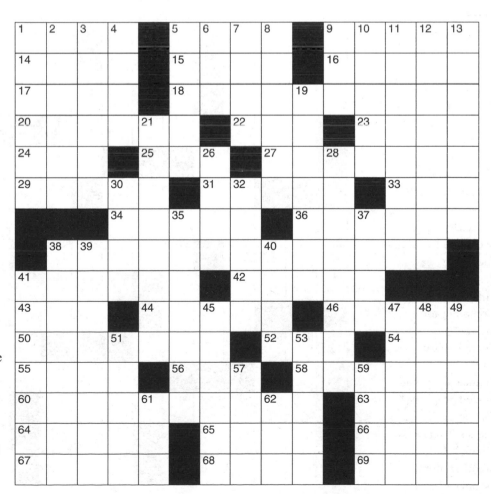

by Stanley Newman

ACROSS

1 "Hell __ no fury . . ."
5 Shout from Scrooge
8 Capital of 71-Across
14 Suffix with switch
15 Life is short and this is long, per Hippocrates
16 Places to sweat it out?
17 Painter Chagall
18 *Restaurant chain known for its coffee and doughnuts
20 Classic fundraising event
22 1950s presidential inits.
23 Writer/illustrator Silverstein
24 Premium theater spot
28 Nobelist William Butler __
32 Spy grp.
33 Word often following "best-case" or "worst-case"
36 Nobody special
40 Arizona tribe
41 Pepsi and Coke
43 __ the Terrible
44 Conundrum
46 Estrange
48 Chick's mother
49 Corporate shuffle, for short
50 Early challenge overcome by Joe Biden
54 Actress Rae of "Insecure"
57 Container for a caterer
58 Some brandy fruits
62 *Pancake topping
66 Seized property, for short
68 Makes flush (with)
69 Greek "H"
70 Weather often associated with Vancouver

71 Place associated with the answers to the starred clues
72 Professor's deg.
73 Village People hit with a spelled-out title

DOWN

1 __ and haw
2 Saudis, e.g.
3 Bar mitzvah text
4 *Leafs-watching time, maybe
5 Cave dwellers
6 "Salome" solo
7 Web designer's code
8 Bear, in un zoológico
9 Road goo
10 Pharaoh known as a "boy king," informally
11 Battery terminal
12 "A Fish Called __"

13 Plus on the balance sheet
19 Lang. in which "peace" is "shalom"
21 Home of the ancient philosopher Zeno
25 Representative Alexandria __-Cortez
26 Mark, as a ballot
27 *Important step after erring
29 Esoteric
30 Spanish uncle
31 Word before system or power
33 __-crab soup
34 Opposite of pro
35 Commercial prefix with Pen
37 Eggs in a lab
38 D.C. player, formerly a Montreal Expo
39 Toronto-to-Montreal dir.
42 Pint at a pub

45 __ Gala (big event in fashion)
47 Guitarist Clapton
50 Poison __
51 Gaily sung syllables
52 Remove, as a brooch
53 Unit of sunshine
55 Cook, as mussels
56 Savory jelly
59 Elite sort of school, for short
60 The "R" of R.B.G.
61 Apple tablet
63 N.Y. airport with many flights to Toronto Pearson
64 Cease
65 Govt. agency for retirees
67 "Cat __ Hot Tin Roof"

by Emma Craven-Matthews

ACROSS

1 Message to the office staff
5 Old South American empire
9 Mosquitoes and gnats
14 Grp. that sets oil benchmarks
15 Start a game of cards
16 American living abroad, e.g.
17 Traveled by subway?
20 Mexican mister
21 Seat at the bar
22 ___ v. Wade
23 Magnum ___ (greatest work)
25 Like a recovering hosp. patient, perhaps
27 "Would you call the elevator for me?"
32 Japanese sash
33 Piece of pizza
34 Foreordained
38 Chrissy of "This Is Us"
40 Pet peeves?
42 Wine region of California
43 Dickens's "___ House"
45 "Naughty" and "nice" things for Santa
47 Letters after nus
48 "Hand me a flashlight"?
51 Admits, as an offense
54 Pouty expression
55 "Well, lookee here!"
56 "Person" that speaks in beeps and boops
60 Home that might melt
63 Use French fries as legal tender?
66 Constellation with a "belt"
67 Good amount of land to build on
68 Golf ball stands
69 Insurance giant
70 Worker paid day by day, maybe
71 Hairstyle that may have a pick

DOWN

1 Cuts the grass
2 Fencing sword
3 Amish cousin
4 Tentacled sea creatures
5 Vow before a judge
6 The latest
7 Jargon
8 Cher, e.g., voicewise
9 Remove, as a sticker
10 Part of an office telephone no.
11 Period of rapid growth
12 It's a no-no
13 Like some ski slopes and prices
18 Pharmacy offerings
19 Certain pueblo dweller
24 ___-evaluation
26 Ending of seven Asian countries' names
27 Item in a purse
28 Whom Cain slew
29 Drawers for money
30 Nail the test
31 Dog walker's need
35 Reason some people move to the Cayman Islands
36 More than amazing
37 Dot's counterpart in Morse code
39 Microwaves
41 Long part of a rose
44 Hurricane that was the subject of 2006's "When the Levees Broke"
46 Keeping a stiff upper lip
49 Any minute now
50 Should, informally
51 Hot après-ski beverage
52 Alternative to Chicago's Midway
53 Put forward, as a theory
57 Dinghy or dory
58 First word of a fairy tale
59 Six years, for a U.S. senator
61 Abbr. on a 0 button
62 ___ buco
64 Sweetie pie
65 Leaf-turning time: Abbr.

by Barbara Lin

ACROSS

1 Swedish group that once comprised two married couples
5 With skill
9 Opening to be filled
12 Sagan who hosted TV's "Cosmos"
13 Like calamari . . . or overloaded circuitry
15 Catches, as a crook
16 Game with Mrs. White and Professor Plum
17 Kendrick with 13 Grammys and a Pulitzer Prize
18 "The Little Rascals" assent
19 Model/TV host on a record five Sports Illustrated Swimsuit Issue covers
22 Envision
23 Top card
24 Skeeves (out)
26 Spirited horse
28 "Grey's Anatomy" actress
30 Snitch (on)
32 Rink surface
33 It has a double helix
34 "Full Frontal" host
38 Dem.'s counterpart
40 Prefix with -phyte or -lithic
41 Down Under hopper, informally
42 North Carolina senator who unseated Elizabeth Dole
45 Kind of tea from India
49 Highly decorative
50 Parts of the body that are "crunched"
52 Blue, e.g. . . . or a rhyme for "blue"
53 Female scholars . . . or a hint to 19-, 28-, 34- and 42-Across
57 Cher or Adele
58 Storehouse of valuables
59 "Pick me, pick me!"

60 Like, for-EV-er
61 See 64-Across
62 __ mortals
63 Fashion monogram
64 With 61-Across, like some typefaces
65 Small wire nail

DOWN

1 Means of entering
2 "Swan Lake," for one
3 Crème __ (dessert)
4 Downwind, at sea
5 Company with a spokesduck
6 Aid for a twisted knee or ankle
7 Result of a twisted ankle
8 Opposite of nah
9 Beverage with a lightning bolt in its logo
10 Leave in the lurch
11 "Gangnam Style" rapper
14 Got close
15 Negative reply to a general
20 __ President
21 G.O.P. color on an election map
25 __ Na Na
27 1970s measure that fell three states short of passing, in brief
28 Not publish yet, as a scoop
29 German's "Alas!"
31 Completely different lines of thought
34 Typical John le Carré work
35 Unionized teachers' grp.
36 Brag
37 Greek goddess of the dawn

38 Studio behind "It's a Wonderful Life"
39 Pincered insects
43 Gaza Strip governing group
44 Devoured
46 Common pronoun pairing
47 Roman goddess of the dawn
48 Intertwined
50 Choreographer Ailey
51 Fortifies, with "up"
54 Metal deposits
55 Places to hold discussions
56 Dead zone?
57 Temp's work unit

by Jessie Bullock and Ross Trudeau

ACROSS

1 Prattle
8 Public square
13 Like records stored for research
15 Popeye's profession
16 Browser's start-up point
17 Buses, as tables
18 Freshly
19 Nonsense
21 Second letter after epsilon
23 Tic-tac-toe win
24 Prohibit
25 Worthless talk
31 Fury
32 Financial claim
33 Hanker (for)
37 Neighs : horses :: __ : sheep
39 Landscaper's tool
42 Raft for a polar bear
43 =
45 It's not odd
47 R.N.'s touch
48 Unintelligible jargon
52 "So that's it!"
55 Itinerary preposition
56 Inexperienced reporter
57 Twaddle
61 Line down the length of a skirt
65 Signing-on info
66 Sudden thought that makes you go "Wow!"
68 Poisons
69 Goes through hurriedly, as during a robbery
70 Jacket alternatives to buttons
71 "Huh?" . . . or a possible response to 1-, 19-, 25-, 48- and 57-Across

DOWN

1 __ Men, group with the 2000 hit "Who Let the Dogs Out"
2 Scientology founder __ Hubbard
3 Highest point
4 Where spiders get their information?
5 Way cool
6 Actress Saint of "North by Northwest"
7 Alternative to Prego
8 1957 title role for Frank Sinatra
9 In __ of (replacing)
10 March goes out like this, as the expression goes
11 "__ the Greek"
12 Pyromaniac's crime
14 Old NASA moon-landing vehicle
15 Great Dane of cartoons, informally
20 Short hairstyle
22 __ Aviv, Israel
25 Match up (with)
26 Baghdad's land
27 Boyfriend
28 Bartlet of "The West Wing" or Clampett of "The Beverly Hillbillies"
29 Figure made by lying in the snow and waving one's arms
30 Sports official, informally
34 Voice below soprano
35 Chocolate/caramel candy
36 Narrow part of a bottle
38 Droop
40 Christmas __ (December 24)
41 Mao Zedong was its leader
44 1960s hippie gatherings
46 Big Apple sch.
49 Hawks and doves
50 Rebuke to a dog
51 "Pygmalion" playwright, for short
52 Borders
53 Wears, as clothes
54 Amazon's virtual assistant
58 Icicles and burning candles both do this
59 __ Lingus
60 Mineral springs
62 Individually
63 Singer/lyricist Paul
64 Classic computer game set on an island
67 "Gangnam Style" singer

by Sarah Keller and Derek Bowman

ACROSS

1 Health resorts
5 Georgia fruit
10 Tuxedo shirt fastener
14 ___ and every
15 Person with a microphone
16 Finest-quality, informally
17 Word after pen or pet
18 Company behind Battlezone and Asteroids
19 "Wheel of Fortune" play
20 Late "Jeopardy!" host Alex
22 V.I.P.'s
24 Quibbles
26 Stack of papers
27 Stand-up comic Margaret
29 "___ whiz!"
30 Approx. when to get to the airport for a pickup
31 Unknown, on a sched.
34 German "mister"
36 "Gnarly, dude!"
38 Bold response to a threat
40 Ready for picking
41 Written material of no consequence
43 Flying: Prefix
44 Enthusiastic response to "Who wants candy?"
46 Internet image file, familiarly
47 Cyclops and Wolverine, for two
48 Title for Paul McCartney or Elton John
49 "The Lord of the Rings" baddie
51 ___ Castellaneta, voice of Homer Simpson
53 "To a Skylark," e.g.
54 Lure of a coffee shop
56 Grouchy Muppet
58 Be sociable
61 Like Satan and some owls
64 BBQ spoiler

65 Supermodel Campbell
67 DVR system
68 Shoestring woe
69 Trio or quartet
70 Rare blood type, for short
71 "The Brady Bunch" threesome
72 German industrial hub
73 Shrek, for one

DOWN

1 Email outbox folder
2 Jack who once hosted "The Tonight Show"
3 Wile E. Coyote's supplier
4 Biblical land with a queen
5 Athlete's goal in competition
6 911 call respondent, for short
7 Hail ___ (cry "Taxi!")
8 Cherry-colored
9 Absolute chicness
10 Malia Obama's sister
11 Quaint greeting
12 Quart, liter or gallon
13 Cozy retreats
21 Tiny bit of work
23 Brown, as a roast
25 One clapping at a circus?
27 Cuomo of CNN
28 Model and TV host Klum
32 Revealed, as one's soul
33 The devout do it on Yom Kippur
35 Big sporting goods retailer
37 Found groovy
39 Honeycomb stuff

42 Relative of Rex or Rover
45 Choice on "Let's Make a Deal"
50 Chocolate beans
52 Sgt., for one
55 Amounts on Monopoly cards
57 "Star Wars" droid, informally
58 Really bugs
59 Prefix meaning "super-tiny"
60 Male turkeys
62 Anytime at all
63 Onetime Venetian V.I.P.
66 U.K. medal accepted and then returned by John Lennon, in brief

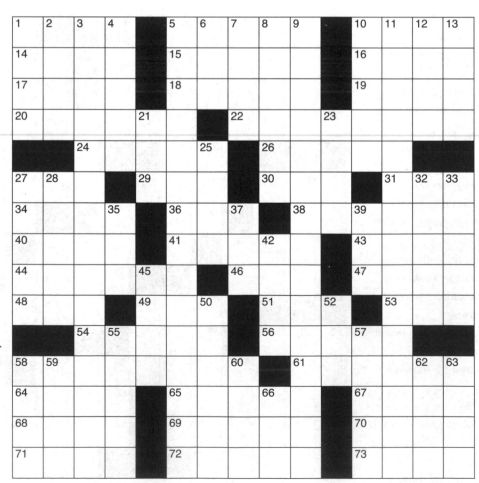

by Alan Massengill and Andrea Carla Michaels

ACROSS

1 Has a long shelf life
6 The Lone Star State
11 Place to recover one's health
14 Native Alaskan
15 Vigilant
16 Arctic diving bird
17 Identity of 61-Across
19 "The X-Files" agcy.
20 Like some reactions and flights during storms
21 Blacktop
23 Opposite of WSW
24 Part of a needle
26 Something a diva may sing
27 Overhaul, as a show
30 Originator of 61-Across
34 Teacher's note accompanying a bad grade, maybe
35 Rapper Shakur
36 Television portrayer of 61-Across
40 Singers Bareilles and Evans
41 Steer clear of
44 Film portrayer of 61-Across
48 Contract stipulation
49 Lead-in to "man" in superhero-dom
50 Flow out, as the tide
52 Youngster
53 Pain in the lower back
57 "Just leave!"
60 Back talk
61 Co-founder of the Justice League
63 Bullring cheer
64 Humdingers
65 Plainly visible
66 Something to write on or crash in
67 Ocular inflammations
68 Smell or taste

DOWN

1 Corporate hierarchies, figuratively
2 Property recipient, in law
3 Rising concern?
4 ___ fish sandwich
5 Linger
6 Late in arriving
7 Inventor Whitney
8 "Hercules" character who got her own show
9 Rainbows, for example
10 Part of an assembly instruction
11 Mac browser
12 Go ___ (become listed on a stock exchange)
13 Japanese dogs
18 "I don't want to hear a ___ out of you!"
22 Meat in many an omelet
25 Teach
28 Adams who played Lois Lane in "Man of Steel"
29 Brainy bunch
31 Tax return pros
32 Batmobile, e.g.
33 Eight-related
35 Poi ingredient
37 Mid-June honoree
38 Longoria of "Desperate Housewives"
39 Some delivery people
42 Weather map lines
43 Easing of international tensions
44 Racehorse's gait
45 Eagle constellation
46 Thrown (together)
47 Shoot the breeze
48 Trucker who relays "bear traps"
51 Confer divine favor on
54 Leather-punching tools
55 Joint malady
56 Just
58 "Terrible" time for tykes
59 Relocate
62 Payment ___

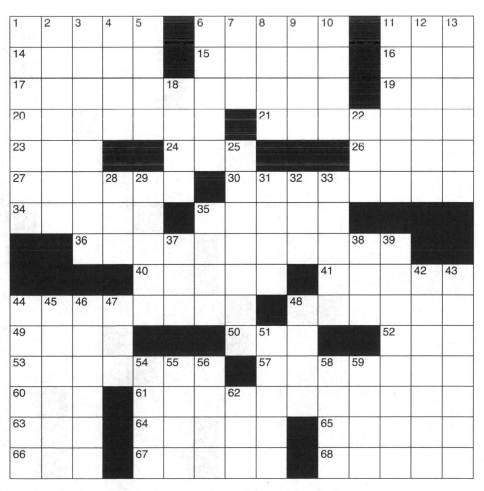

by Kathy Wienberg

ACROSS

1 Periodically sold fast-food item
6 What melting ice cream cones do
10 Swindle
14 Actress Donovan of "Sabrina the Teenage Witch"
15 "Othello" villain
16 House in Mexico
17 Less risky
18 Cast celebration at the end of filming
20 Feelers
22 Frozen expanse
23 Olive ___ (Popeye's sweetie)
24 It can be used for welcoming or wrestling
25 Charged particle
26 Souvenirs from Havana
31 Loosen, as laces
32 CPR performer
33 Occupants of kennels
37 Subjects in which women have traditionally been underrepresented, for short
38 Letters between thetas and kappas
40 Human rights attorney Clooney
41 FX network's "___ of Anarchy"
42 Mediterranean, e.g.
43 Prenatal test, for short
44 Going from nightspot to nightspot
47 Soccer star Hamm
50 Buffoon
51 "___ you serious?"
52 Worker just for a summer, maybe
54 Source of healthful fat and fiber
59 Certain online board for discussion of a topic
61 Like an angle less than 90°

62 Old Russian ruler
63 Brontë's "Jane ___"
64 Ethical
65 Divisions of tennis matches
66 Rocker Lou
67 Popular vodka brand, for short

DOWN

1 Flat-topped hill
2 Extended family
3 Break in relations
4 "Understood"
5 Without exception . . . as in dry counties?
6 Hindu festival of lights
7 Hard to find
8 Supermarket chain that's big in small towns
9 Breakfast treats from a toaster
10 Read over
11 Rap's ___ B
12 Member of a major-league team with a name that's out of this world?
13 Like an early Central American civilization
19 "Nobody ___ Baby in a corner" (line from "Dirty Dancing")
21 Big Apple inits.
24 One of a baby's first words
26 Talk a blue streak?
27 "Do ___ others . . ."
28 Vitamin also known as PABA
29 Goals
30 Do better than average, gradewise
33 Like a just-used towel

34 Hilton alternative
35 Profit
36 Trudge
38 Bahamian or Fijian
39 Egg: Fr.
43 Ways to earn college credits while in H.S.
44 Part of a reactor
45 Stopped
46 60 minuti
47 Sprays
48 Occupied
49 Chance for a hit
53 Blunders
54 Command to a cannoneer
55 Edinburgh native
56 Continental currency
57 And others: Abbr.
58 Where you might find the starts of 18-, 26-, 44- and 59-Across
60 Easter egg colorer

by Martha Kimes

ACROSS

1 Get ready to hem, say
6 Hankering
10 Thomas Edison's middle name
14 Boxing venue
15 __ Hari (W.W. I spy)
16 Russian "no"
17 City where you won't find the Eiffel Tower
19 Cotton processors
20 Not to mention . . .
21 Org. for which Jason Bourne works in "The Bourne Identity"
22 Author Charlotte, Emily or Anne
24 City where you won't find the Parthenon
28 1965 Alabama march site
30 Saintly "Mother"
31 Utopian
32 Plant on a trellis
33 1950s White House nickname
36 "Nuts!"
37 Gets ready, as for surgery
39 Insect flying in a cloud
40 CPR pro
41 Sound made by helicopter rotors
42 Rings, as a church bell
43 Yasir of the P.L.O.
45 What the back of a store might open onto
46 City where you won't find Virgil's Tomb
50 Pal of Jerry on "Seinfeld"
51 Driveway material
52 QB successes
55 Excessive drinking or gambling
56 City where you won't find the El Greco Museum
60 Neck and neck
61 Cousin of "Kapow!"
62 Refrigerator compound
63 Cincinnati squad
64 "Well, that was stupid of me!"
65 Commuter boat

DOWN

1 Owner of the first bed that Goldilocks tested
2 Tehran's land
3 "Here comes Poindexter!"
4 Prefix with lateral or cellular
5 Easter-related
6 "Let me rephrase that . . ."
7 Receipt line just above the total
8 Org. that runs Windy City trains
9 Fading stars
10 Kind of goat that's the source of mohair
11 Not upstanding, in either sense of the word
12 20-ounce size at Starbucks
13 Confounded
18 Bit of attire you might learn how to put on while using a mirror
23 Valentine's Day flower
25 I.R.S. agent, quaintly
26 More than a couple
27 Part of a golf club
28 Pro or con, in a debate
29 Dutch cheese
33 All riled up
34 Curly-leafed cabbage
35 Online market for craftspeople
37 What follows the initial part of a master plan
38 Repeated bit in jazz
39 Neuter, as a horse
41 Small, brown bird
42 Join in couples
43 1986 sci-fi sequel set in deep space
44 Venerated symbols
46 "Not a chance!"
47 Still surviving
48 Walked nervously back and forth
49 Far out
53 Designer Christian
54 __ Pictures, one of Hollywood's Big Five studios
57 Cry of surprise
58 Drink like a cat
59 Bauxite, e.g.

by Jeff Stillman

ACROSS

1 Modern Persia
5 Arnaz who loved Lucy
9 Become acclimated
14 "Finding ___" (2003 Pixar film)
15 Alternative to a wood, in golf
16 Name said twice before "Wherefore art thou"
17 In vogue
18 Oscar the Grouch's home
20 International Court of Justice location, with "The"
22 Bulls in a bullfight
23 Old weapon in hand-to-hand combat
26 Place for a nest
30 Digital picture, maybe
31 Less fresh
33 Emergency call in Morse code
36 Wild guess
39 With 60-Across, one of two U.S. vice presidents to resign from office
40 Result of a football blitz, maybe
44 Completely anesthetized
45 Exercise that might be done on a mat
46 Cover gray, perhaps
47 Like vinegar
49 "Holy moly!"
52 English channel, informally, with "the"
53 Bit of fashionable footwear
58 Home in the shape of a dome
60 See 39-Across
62 Dreaded cry from a boss . . . or a hint to the ends of 18-, 23-, 40- and 53-Across
67 Listing in a travel guide
68 Texas ___ (school NW of Houston)
69 Dealer in futures?
70 It's a plot!
71 News media
72 Rival of Harvard
73 Wood for boat decks

DOWN

1 Not give an ___ (be stubborn)
2 Give a makeover, informally
3 Spanish girlfriend
4 "Hey, don't jump in front of me in the line!"
5 Insult
6 Time span sometimes named after a president
7 Rather, informally
8 Where work may pile up
9 Best Picture winner set in 1-Across
10 Swims at the Y, say
11 "The Walking Dead" network
12 Cause of a sleepless night for a princess, in a fairy tale
13 Whole bunch
19 Greek counterpart of Mars
21 Yadda, yadda, yadda
24 Zap with a light beam
25 Contest attempt
27 Classic work that's the basis for Shakespeare's "Troilus and Cressida"
28 "Goodness gracious!"
29 Not having two nickels to rub together
32 "For shame!"
33 Fledgling pigeon
34 Weight whose abbreviation ends in a "z," oddly
35 "Sexy" lady in a Beatles song
37 Blood grouping system
38 Hole-some breakfast food?
41 Nickname for the Cardinals, with "the"
42 Prefix with -pod or -partite
43 Zoo enclosure
48 Foal : mare :: ___ : cow
50 Lawyers' org.
51 Took care of someone else's pooch
54 Loud
55 Land with a demilitarized zone
56 Delayed
57 Four: Prefix
59 Insets in a crown
61 Line on a calendar
62 Talk, talk, talk
63 Regatta implement
64 French "a"
65 Wriggly fish
66 Dr. of hip-hop

by Kevin Christian and Andrea Carla Michaels

ACROSS

1 Entry in a doctor's calendar: Abbr.
5 Thanksgiving vegetable
8 100, gradewise
13 Rage
14 "Early in life, I had learned that if you want something, you had better __ some noise": Malcolm X
15 Take care of
16 Journey
17 Jessica of "Fantastic Four"
18 Reeves of "The Matrix"
19 One on the front lines during a crisis
22 Do a new production of, as a recording
23 Alternative to carpeting
24 "You bet!"
25 Became a millionaire, say
29 "It's __ of the times"
33 Finish first in a race
34 Factory-inspecting org.
35 Crown wearer at a fall football game
39 Bullets and such
40 Since, informally
41 Turn topsy-turvy
42 Tight embrace
44 Advanced deg. for a writer or musician
46 Hair tamer
47 __ Trench (deepest point on earth)
52 Unmanned Dept. of Defense aircraft
56 Rob
57 With 58-Across, collective consciousness . . . or a hint to the ends of 19-, 35- and 52-Across
58 See 57-Across
59 "Beats me!"
60 Qatari leader
61 Lake bordering Cleveland
62 Kick up __ (be unruly)
63 Web portal with a butterfly logo
64 Bucks and does

DOWN

1 ". . . happily ever __"
2 Prize money
3 Light beam splitter
4 Like a go-go-go personality
5 Certain New Haven collegians
6 "Allahu __!" (Muslim cry)
7 Brunch, e.g.
8 Invite on a date
9 One's equals
10 Faucet problem
11 __ Reader (magazine with the slogan "Cure ignorance")
12 Like lemons
14 Dull photo finish
20 "Bye Bye Bye" boy band
21 Incorrect
25 __ and tonic
26 "Understood"
27 Fifth-most-common family name in China
28 Round of applause
29 "Moby-Dick" captain
30 A few
31 "__ Be" (2010 #1 hit by the Black Eyed Peas)
32 Raphael Warnock and Jon Ossoff, for two
33 Rapper __ Khalifa
36 Circular windows
37 Popular gift shop purchase
38 Actor Dennis
43 Greetings
44 Singer Gaye
45 Cooking device in a fast-food restaurant
47 Injures
48 Ready for battle
49 Bête __
50 "Little Orphan __"
51 Passover observance
52 __-certified organic
53 Double __ Oreos
54 DoorDash list
55 Not us

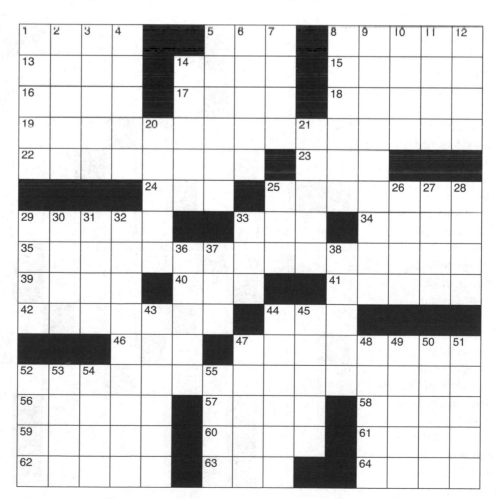

by Soleil Saint-Cyr

ACROSS

1 Actress/TV host ___ Pinkett Smith
5 The five weekdays, for short
10 33⅓ r.p.m. records
13 Satan's doings
14 One who's habitually afraid
16 Constitutional proposal supported by the National Woman's Party, for short
17 "Scenter" of the face
18 Musical key with three flats
19 ___ Man ("The Wizard of Oz" character)
20 "You did it!"
22 Wandered off
24 "Without further ___ . . ."
25 Harp-shaped constellation
27 Annual science fiction awards
28 China's Chairman ___
30 Snake in "Antony and Cleopatra"
32 Ballyhoos
34 Celestial bodies
36 Like the newest gadgetry, informally
38 No longer employed: Abbr.
39 Winnie-the-___
40 J'___ (Dior perfume)
41 Very
42 Banned pollutant, in brief
43 Lead-in to -stat
44 "Ant-Man and the ___" (2018 film)
45 Relative of a steam bath
47 Narrow inlet
48 Actor Mahershala
49 City NNW of Detroit
51 Times before eves, in ads
53 Deliverer of a noted speech upon the death of Martin Luther King Jr. (4/4/1968), in brief
56 February 29

58 Acquired lots of, as money
60 ___-country (music genre)
61 Music genre for Billie Eilish
63 Dog in Oz
64 Cry to a toreador
65 Monster slain by Perseus
66 Nincompoop
67 Unhappy
68 Tirades
69 St. ___ Bay, Jamaica

DOWN

1 Liz's best friend on "30 Rock"
2 Shun
3 Completely confused
4 Away from the wind, at sea
5 "Star Trek" doctor
6 Lara Croft, in film
7 Conflict in 2017's "Wonder Woman," in brief
8 Light browns
9 Foam
10 "Loosen up!" . . . or a hint to this puzzle's circled letters
11 "High" figure in a tarot deck
12 Beach composition
15 Noted sex therapist
21 Musical artist "from the block," familiarly
23 In the past
26 Queens neighborhood
29 What's left in a fireplace
31 Layer of soil that never thaws
33 Octagonal street sign
34 Antonyms: Abbr.
35 Record label co-founded by Jay-Z
36 "That'll be the day!"
37 Corp. V.I.P.
41 Messenger bird in the Harry Potter books
43 Bicycle built for two
46 Tiny bite
48 Question
50 Horse whisperer, e.g.
52 Patatas bravas, calamares and others
54 Naturally belong
55 They may be hard to untie
56 Vientiane's land
57 Who says "When you look at the dark side, careful you must be"
59 "At Last" singer James
62 Wordplay joke

by Portia Lundie

ACROSS

1 Dance at a Jewish wedding
5 Chemical that burns
9 Chevrolet muscle car
15 Home of Waikiki Beach
16 Capital of Italia
17 Brought (in), as a fish
18 Vittles
19 "What __ goes!" (parent's pronouncement)
20 Task to "run"
21 "Rush Hour" and "21 Jump Street" [Clinton]
24 Handle with __
25 Friends' opposite
26 TV deputy of Mayberry [Bush 43]
30 Leave out
34 Kind of port on a computer, in brief
35 Zig or zag
36 Anticipate
38 Dines
40 The Buddha is often depicted meditating under it [Obama]
43 Numerical information
44 Windsurfing locale NE of Honolulu
46 "Superfruit" berry
48 Cousin of "Kapow!"
49 Boxer Spinks who upset Muhammad Ali
50 C-D-E-F-G-A-B-C, e.g. [Biden]
53 Linguist Chomsky
55 Small amounts
56 What the starts of 21-, 26-, 40- and 50-Across are, for the presidents in their clues
63 Prayer beads
64 Shoe bottom
65 More than magnificent
68 Smitten
69 __ of Arendelle (Disney queen)
70 Device that makes a TV "smart"
71 Combs to add volume, as a stylist might
72 Not the passive sort
73 Part of a stairway

DOWN

1 Go __-wild
2 Means of propelling a boat
3 Baked dessert made with tart red stalks (and loads of sugar)
4 University that's also a color
5 Really dry
6 Cloth used to cover a teapot, to Brits
7 Apple on a desktop
8 Respite from work
9 __ brûlée (French custard)
10 Spray can mist
11 __ Griffin Enterprises
12 Jai __
13 Actress Russo
14 Probability
22 Mosquito repellent ingredient
23 Author Edgar Allan __
24 Like Friday attire in some offices
26 Play music in the subway, perhaps
27 Rhyming title character who plays the tuba in Cuba, in a Rudy Vallee song
28 Curly hairstyle, for short
29 1099-__ (bank-issued tax form)
31 Plenty steamed
32 Stuck, with no way out
33 Sums
36 Orchard fruit
37 Identify
39 __-mo
41 Howard's best friend on "The Big Bang Theory"
42 "Green" prefix
45 Rattle
47 "What __ be done?"
50 Founder of Communist China
51 Made smile
52 Basketball players, quaintly
54 "You got that right!"
56 Legal order
57 Sharpen
58 __ Verde (locale of San Juan's airport)
59 Tourist town in northern New Mexico
60 By oneself
61 "If all __ fails . . ."
62 Letter starter
66 Prez with the pooch Heidi
67 Saucer go-with

by Meconya Alford

ACROSS

1 Players in a play
5 In a while
9 One of thousands in a Rose Bowl float
14 Prussia's ___ von Bismarck
15 Fat-removing surgery, for short
16 Extreme pain
17 Caboose's location
18 Ode or sonnet
19 Shrink in fear
20 "Jeez, lighten up, will ya!"
23 Ram's mate
24 How extraterrestrials come, we hope
25 Think (over)
27 U.S. intelligence org.
28 Bombarded, as with questions
32 Ham it up
35 Score in hockey
36 Black-tie charity event, maybe
37 Sprinted
38 As expected
39 Long-running CBS drama
40 The "I" of I.M.F.: Abbr.
42 Abode in Aachen
43 Earns
45 Pieces of evidence in court
47 Grammy winner ___ Nas X
48 Replacement for the lira and mark
49 Faux fireplace items
53 U.S.S.R. intelligence org.
55 Like medical expenses you pay for yourself
58 Long (for)
60 What a wheel connects to
61 Author/journalist Quindlen
62 Cove
63 Order to someone holding a deck of cards
64 Game suggested by the ends of 20-, 38- and 55-Across and 11- and 34-Down
65 On/off device
66 Fare for aardvarks
67 Letters on love letters

DOWN

1 Welsh ___ (dog)
2 Had dinner at home
3 It may say "Forever"
4 Suffering
5 Andean animal valued for its wool
6 Mythical woman after whom element 41 is named
7 Abbr. below "0" on a phone
8 Iditarod terminus
9 Get stuff ready to go
10 Bigheadedness
11 Bar from the bathroom?
12 Once more
13 Muse's instrument
21 "At ___, soldier!"
22 Enough
26 Turkey drumstick, e.g.
28 Hocus-___
29 Évian and Perrier
30 Alternatively
31 Speaker's platform
32 Great Lake with the smallest volume
33 Tail-less cat
34 Alert
35 Insect you may swat away
38 State school SE of Columbus, in brief
41 Lucy of TV's "Elementary"
43 Kind of soup often served at a sushi bar
44 Sign of online shouting
46 Literary Emily or Charlotte
47 Places for tiny U.S. flags
49 Key for Debussy's "La fille aux cheveux de lin"
50 "All righty then . . ."
51 Italian city known for its salami
52 What holds up an ear of corn
53 Ukraine's capital, to Ukrainians
54 Actress Rowlands
56 "Look what I did!"
57 Animals in a yoke
59 Gun, as an engine

by Barbara Lin

ACROSS

1 Unruly throng
4 Houston team
10 Sound heard in a long hallway, maybe
14 "__ Father who art in heaven . . ."
15 Engages in thievery
16 Emotional state
17 Baton Rouge sch.
18 *Seattle, 1962
20 "And you?," to Caesar
22 Queries
23 Photos at the dentist's
24 Happen next
26 Pigs' digs
27 *Paris, 1889
31 Partook of a meal
34 Wake others up while you sleep, perhaps
35 Ostensible
37 100%
38 Theme park with an "Imagination!" pavilion
40 Mont Blanc and Matterhorn
41 "Why didn't I think of that!"
43 Laudable Lauder
44 Salt Lake City athlete
45 *Chicago, 1893
48 "__ appétit!"
49 More recent
50 Word before shell or mail
53 Rock band that electrifies audiences?
55 Dull-colored
58 Events for which the answers to the three starred clues were built
61 Jack Nicholson's weapon in "The Shining"
62 Burn soother
63 The "P" in UPS
64 "__ get you!"
65 Wanders (about)
66 Like some college bros
67 After tax

DOWN

1 Undercover operative
2 Remove from power
3 Inelegant problem-solving technique
4 Nincompoop
5 One of the Twin Cities
6 Cups, saucers, pot, etc.
7 Eight lamb chops, typically, or a frame for 15 pool balls
8 Cheers at a fútbol match
9 Nine-digit government ID
10 Manicurist's board
11 Musical finale
12 Sacred
13 Lyric poems
19 Like a 10th or 11th inning, in baseball
21 Not at liberty
25 Visualize
26 Sunni or Shia, in Islam
27 TV channel for college sports
28 Arctic native
29 __ the Grouch
30 Ply with chocolates and roses, say
31 Kind of vehicle to take off-road
32 Shelter that might be made of buffalo skin
33 '50s Ford flop
36 Made a verbal attack, with "out"
38 Garden of earthly delights
39 Pay-__-view
42 Words spoken after a big raise?
43 "Yu-u-uck!"
46 Charge with a crime
47 Hush-hush
48 Gymnast Simone
50 Promotional goodies handed out at an event
51 The Big Easy, in brief
52 Three-time A.L. M.V.P. (2003, 2005 and 2007), informally
53 Miles away
54 Sweetheart, in Salerno
56 One of several on a tractor-trailer
57 Pants holder-upper
59 Tanning lotion stat
60 Sneaky

by Michael Lieberman

ACROSS

1 Schoolyard friend
9 Strolled
15 Abandon
16 Percussion item that's shaken
17 Manufacturing of factory goods, e.g.
18 Victimize
19 Ace of spades or queen of hearts
20 Biblical twin of Jacob
22 Existence
23 Before, poetically
24 "__ Beso" (1962 Paul Anka hit)
25 Shared with, as a story
27 Sandwich often served with mayo
28 Connector between levels of a fire station
29 "I'm shocked!," in a text
31 Religion based in Haifa, Israel
34 Sulk
35 Bothered state
36 "What goes up must come down," e.g.
37 NPR host Shapiro
38 Big name in transmission repair
39 Young lady
40 U.S. sports org. with many prominent Korean champions
41 Gown
42 The Monkees' "__ Believer"
43 Catch sight of
44 Org. in "Zero Dark Thirty"
45 Noted children's research hospital
47 Actor Philip with a star on the Hollywood Walk of Fame
48 Uncle __ (patriotic figure)
51 Dragon in "The Hobbit"
52 Legendary queen and founder of Carthage
54 Change domiciles
55 Tasket's partner in a nursery rhyme
57 Hazards for offshore swimmers
59 Go to
60 Faucet attachments
61 Writings of Ph.D. candidates
62 X-axis

DOWN

1 Y-axis
2 Moon-related
3 Tennis's Agassi
4 "__ be surprised"
5 Greek M's
6 Swear (to)
7 Middle part of the body
8 One-named Irish singer
9 Bit of concert equipment
10 Stone for a statue
11 One of over 200 recognized by the American Kennel Club
12 "I'm listening"
13 Subject of this puzzle
14 "Nuts!"
21 Golden state?
24 "Night" memoirist Wiesel
26 Cheer at a bullfight
27 Sacks
28 "__ and Bess"
30 Classic Pontiac sports cars
31 Much-visited Indonesian isle
32 "Father" of 13-Down
33 Tries some food
34 Drew for an atlas
35 Singer Bareilles
38 Tennis score after deuce
40 '60s hallucinogenic
43 Playwright O'Neill
44 Actress Priyanka who was 2000's Miss World
46 Fakes out of position, as in football
47 Farewell
48 "Me too"
49 Prevent, as disaster
50 Complicated, as a divorce
51 "A.S.A.P.!"
53 Baghdad's land
54 Baseball glove
56 Football scores, for short
58 Lie in the sun

by Eric Bornstein

ACROSS

1 Vehicles on snow-covered hills
6 Watering place for a camel
11 Indoor animal
14 "The Fox and the Grapes" storyteller
15 Trick-taking card game
16 Messenger __
17 Large bird of prey with a brownish-yellow neck
19 Suffix with cynic or skeptic
20 Pleased
21 Hombre
22 Pool stick
23 Make excited, as a crowd
26 Smooshed into compact layers
28 __ carte (ordered separately)
29 Blue race in "Avatar"
31 Kind of pickle
32 __ for tat
33 Actor Kevin whose last name shares four letters with his first
35 Eric Clapton hit that's over seven minutes long
38 Light bulb unit
40 Butchers' offerings
42 Like tops and tales
43 Speak extemporaneously
45 Boringly proper
47 Conclude
48 Greek god of love
50 Away from the wind, nautically
51 It's just a number, they say
52 Single, double and triple, on the diamond
55 Shows mercy to
57 Plant bristle
58 Poet's "before"
59 Olla podrida, for one
60 Sheep's cry

61 Where you can find a 17-Across perched on an 11-Down devouring a 25-Down
66 Noah's construction
67 Opening remarks
68 One of the Allman Brothers
69 Envision
70 Valuable item
71 New York's Memorial __ Kettering Cancer Center

DOWN

1 Droop
2 Zodiac sign before Virgo
3 Course for some immigrants, in brief
4 Historic Kansas fort name
5 Explore caves
6 Like debts
7 "Bingo!"
8 Letter after rho
9 Cuba or Aruba
10 Sign maker's pattern
11 Cactus with an edible fruit
12 Follow as a consequence
13 No longer feral
18 Incendiary bomb material
23 Formal ruling on a point of Islamic law
24 Trojan War epic poem
25 Venomous predator with a vibrating tail
26 They get smashed at parties
27 "Sadly . . ."
30 Strives for victory
34 And others: Abbr.
36 Sudden forward thrust

37 World's longest continental mountain range
39 Lose stamina
41 Afternoon nap
44 European region that lent its name to a nonconforming lifestyle
46 "Could be . . ."
49 Ambulance sounds
52 Rum-soaked desserts
53 In the loop
54 Messages that sometimes contain emojis
56 Really, really bad
59 Get off __-free
62 Fury
63 Philosopher __-tzu
64 Get __ on (ace)
65 Four-star officer: Abbr.

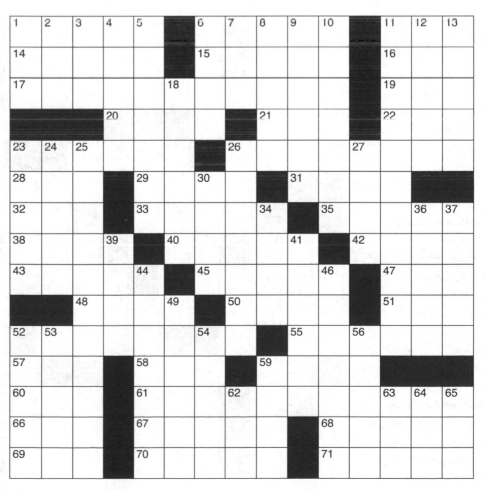

by Philip K. Chow

ACROSS

1 Quick punch
4 Submitted a résumé
11 Old-fashioned record collection, for short
14 Friend in France
15 Comedian Jimmy who joked of his "schnozzola"
16 The "A" of I.P.A.
17 Collectible toy vehicle
19 Long-bodied jazz instrument, for short
20 Mother hen's responsibility
21 Mil. branch with dress blues and dress whites
23 Couch
24 Bygone Swedish auto
27 Energy-efficient illumination sources, for short
29 Birthplace of General Motors
33 Nosy sort
34 Flowing, musically
35 Those who are not among us (or are they?)
38 Locale for the radius and ulna
39 Family
40 Use needle and thread
41 "Here, you'll like it!"
43 Prefix with red or structure
45 Certain online dating bio
48 No more than
49 Yanks' opponents in the Civil War
50 Plummet
53 Birdsong
56 Sierra ___ (African land)
57 Predicament
58 1980 Stephen King novel . . . or a hint to the beginnings of 17-, 29- and 45-Across
62 Preceding, poetically
63 Flipped (out)
64 Squid's defense
65 "You called?"
66 Glittery dress adornments
67 Investments with account nos.

DOWN

1 Door parts
2 Bitter Italian liqueur
3 Removed with the teeth
4 Condition that affects concentration, for short
5 Stop on a drinker's "crawl"
6 Expert
7 Not stringently enforcing the rules
8 Nighttime demons
9 Greek letters that rhyme with three other letters
10 Laura with an Oscar and an Emmy
11 So-called "Sin City"
12 Tots' time together
13 Health class subject
18 Classic eyes for Frosty
22 Prank interviewer who referred to Buzz Aldrin as "Buzz Lightyear"
24 Person who might bother a bedmate
25 Elemental part of an element
26 Band aid
28 Contents of some drifts
30 Imbecilic
31 White ___ of Dover
32 Artist Matisse
35 Famous almost-last words from Caesar
36 Security alarm trigger
37 They establish order in language classes
39 Door part
42 Skunk funk
43 Rageaholic's state
44 Tree in the birch family
46 Algebra, for calc, e.g.
47 Like art that might offend prudish sorts
51 Without interruption
52 Corner offices and prime parking spots, for company V.I.P.'s
54 Tightest of pals, in brief
55 Old Italian money
56 Blokes
57 Funny Tina
59 ___ de vie
60 Hit the slopes
61 Point value for a "Z" in Scrabble

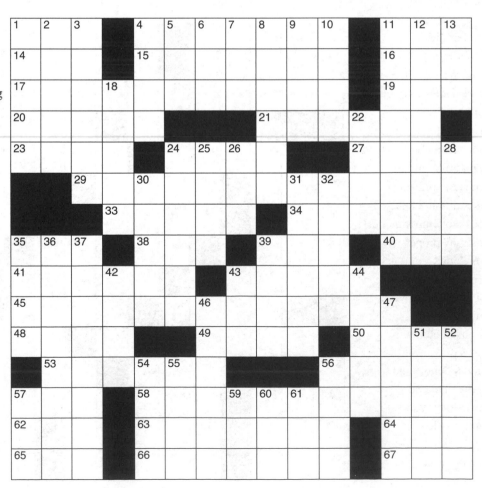

by Daniel Grinberg

ACROSS

1 Fighting, as countries
6 Team sport with scrums
11 Naked ___ jaybird
14 Stage of development
15 Writer Zola
16 Fractional amt.
17 Equestrian outfit
19 Part of a chem class
20 Lie snugly
21 Perfect example
23 French friend
24 Take a lo-o-ong bath
26 Home plate officials, informally
27 Minor job at a body shop
29 Children's character who lives in a briar patch
33 Not bottled or canned, as beer
35 Word that might be "proper"
36 Hamlet's dilemma . . . with a phonetic hint for the last words of 17- and 29-Across and the first words of 45- and 63-Across
42 ___ vera
43 Wedding or parade
45 "E-G-B-D-F" musical symbol
51 Voice below mezzo-soprano
52 Schemer against Othello
53 What the Supremes said to do "in the name of love"
55 Test for an advanced deg. seeker
56 Requirement for sainthood
60 Peninsula with Oman and Yemen
62 Suffix with Sudan or Japan
63 California golf resort that has hosted six U.S. Opens
66 Tennis do-over
67 Garlicky sauce

68 Slow, musically
69 Units on a football field: Abbr.
70 One who laughs "Ho, ho, ho!"
71 Beginning

DOWN

1 Mo. with many (not so) happy returns?
2 Popular Girl Scout cookie
3 Undertake with gusto
4 Buyer's warning
5 Monopoly payments
6 Try, try again?
7 Actress Thurman
8 Taunt
9 Spot on a radar screen
10 Supposed source of mysterious footprints in the Himalayas
11 Self-assurance
12 Shrimp ___ (seafood dish)
13 Optimally
18 Amorphous lump
22 Place to take a bath
23 Kerfuffle
25 Shelters for shelties
28 Run one's mouth
30 Outback hopper, informally
31 Routine that one might get stuck in
32 Pay to play
34 Ring, as church bells
37 Mississippi's ___ Miss
38 Huge bird of lore
39 In vitro fertilization needs
40 Citizens of Brussels and Antwerp

41 Theatergoer's break
44 What a ballerina twirls on
45 At just the right moment
46 Made a higher poker bet
47 White wetlands birds
48 ___ constrictor
49 And others: Lat.
50 Shout after an errant drive
54 Artist Picasso
57 Tax pros, for short
58 "Star Wars" princess
59 Black, in poetry
61 Has-___
64 Toasted sandwich, familiarly
65 All the rage

by Lynn Lempel

ACROSS

1 Animal that barks
4 Bourbon barrel material
7 Tribal leader
12 Blunder
13 ___ colada
15 List for a meeting
16 *Certain psychedelic experience
18 Nintendo game featuring balance exercises
19 ___ of the game
20 Early auto engine's power source
22 Construction area, e.g.
23 Performs like Iggy Azalea
25 Social stratum
27 Provoke
30 Nevada city on the Truckee River
31 PC monitor type, in brief
34 *Hairstyle popularized by Lucille Ball
36 Hip-hop producer who founded Aftermath Entertainment
38 For two, in music
39 Jeans material
41 At the drop of ___ (instantly)
42 Drops in the mail
44 *Cheap neighborhood bar
46 Bygone Mach 1 breaker, for short
47 Major water line
49 Hang around idly
50 "Wanna join us?"
52 Fairy tale bear with a hard bed
53 Delivery room instruction
55 Put on hold
57 Religious sisters
61 Real lowlife
63 "So there!" . . . or what you can do to the ends of the answers to the starred clues?

65 Looks without blinking
66 Ship personnel
67 Number of Q tiles in Scrabble
68 Item that may be baked or mashed, informally
69 Caustic solution
70 Ingredient in a Denver omelet

DOWN

1 College faculty head
2 Whale that preys on octopuses
3 Worrisome, as news
4 Make a pick
5 Cockpit reading
6 Makes a scarf, say
7 FX in much sci-fi and fantasy
8 Bank holdup

9 *Bunt single, e.g.
10 Heading in a word processing menu
11 Destiny
14 Gibbon or gorilla
15 "Geez, that sucks!"
17 Expressed contempt for
21 Like vinegar
24 Falcons, on scoreboards
26 Roll for a greenskeeper
27 "No bid from me"
28 Connection points
29 *Home of many a courthouse
30 Talk too long
32 Yearn for
33 Scare off
35 Pop singer Dion
37 Visibly elated
40 Nonsense

43 Home of the George W. Bush Institute, in brief
45 Hack (off)
48 Capitol Hill staffers
51 Busiest airport in the Midwest
52 Oyster's creation
53 "Hey, over here!"
54 ___ Beauty (Sephora competitor)
56 Org. that monitors consumer scams
58 "Here comes trouble . . ."
59 Mama's mama
60 Part of a cherry you don't eat
62 Gen ___ (millennial's follower)
64 Ovine mother

by Zhouqin Burnikel

ACROSS

1 Things that justify the means, some say
5 Eight: Sp.
9 Rampaging groups
13 Hoedown locale
14 "Moby-Dick" captain
15 Feverish fit
16 Cinnamon buns and such
19 Community-maintained website
20 Person from Bangkok
21 Disney character loosely based on Hans Christian Andersen's "Snow Queen"
23 "Hmm, that's not good . . ."
25 Slight coloring
27 Slight downturn
28 Modern pet name
29 Cyclical paradox discussed in "Gödel, Escher, Bach"
32 Societal problems
34 Brain reading, for short
35 Touches one's chin and moves the hand down to say "Thank you," for example
36 Recipe amt.
38 ___ and crafts
40 "Shucks!"
43 Bar serving
44 The "A" of I.R.A.: Abbr.
48 Onetime TV political drama set in Washington
52 "Now I get it!"
53 Tit for ___
54 Mike of TV's "Dirty Jobs" and "Somebody's Gotta Do It"
55 Strategy
57 Yours: Fr.
59 Potato accompanier in soup
61 Shopping center
62 Sports metaphor used to describe esoteric knowledge . . . with a hint to the circled letters
66 Cinema showing
67 Amateur mag
68 1998 Sarah McLachlan hit
69 Ladder rung
70 Jazzy James
71 Forest feline

DOWN

1 Flow back, as the tide
2 Tusked marine animal
3 Spinning top with a Hebrew letter on each side
4 Type not to be trusted
5 Fumbler
6 Informal conversation
7 #, on social media
8 Procure
9 China's ___ Zedong
10 Eye creepily
11 Yale's Handsome Dan mascot, for one
12 Time spent with a psychiatrist, e.g.
17 Optimas and Souls, in the auto world
18 Good thing to have on hand at a wedding?
22 TikTok and Fitbit, for two
23 Kimono sash
24 GPS suggestions: Abbr.
26 Rorschach, for one
30 Street cred
31 Simpson who is a Buddhist and a vegetarian
33 Hearty bowlful
37 Bar serving
38 Heavyweight champ known as "The Greatest"
39 Figure in home economics?
40 Lead-in to boy or girl
41 Hypothetical musings
42 "Now, work!"
43 Slightly
45 Purr-son who loves her pets?
46 Doin' nothin'
47 Tic-___-toe
49 Last word at an auction
50 Pluck, as an eyebrow
51 Charades or dominoes
56 Scheming group
58 ___ of Skye
60 Philosopher Immanuel
63 Little troublemaker
64 South China ___
65 Opposite of strict

by Aimee Lucido and Ella Dershowitz

ACROSS

1 Opening made by a letter opener
5 Antifur org.
9 Wee bit
14 Old-fashioned fight club?
15 Wrinkle remover
16 Pacific Island group that was once a setting for "Survivor"
17 New couple, in a gossip column
18 Look after, as a fire, bar or flock
19 1940s nuclear event, for short
20 "I'm willing to pay that amount"
23 "___ Just Not That Into You" (2009 rom-com)
24 New newt
25 Get value from
26 "Law & Order" spinoff, informally
27 Longtime advertiser at the Indy 500
29 Oolong or Darjeeling
32 "If I can be honest here . . ."
37 Submarine device
38 The "A" of E.T.A.: Abbr.
39 Main line from the heart
40 "Absolutely! 100% positive!"
43 E.R. staffers
44 Snake symbolizing old Egyptian royalty
45 Gives a thumbs-up
46 Transmission by telephone
48 ___ alai
49 Pennies: Abbr.
52 20-, 32- or 40-Across
58 Boots from political office
59 Southwestern tribe with a snake dance
60 Start of every California ZIP code
61 How a ballerina often dances
62 Israeli statesman Abba ___
63 Historical novelist Seton
64 Jumped
65 Alternative to a drumstick
66 Historical

DOWN

1 Actress Dame Maggie
2 Woodworker's tool
3 Drinks akin to Slush Puppies
4 Work as a sub
5 Pathetic
6 Put up, as a monument
7 Muscular firmness
8 "___ Love Her" (Beatles ballad)
9 Practices jabs and hooks
10 TV journalist Couric
11 Fashion designer Cassini
12 Bit of attire that might say "MISS UNIVERSE"
13 Jabba the ___
21 Paul who went on a midnight ride
22 Building manager, for short
26 Wild guess
27 Razor sharpener at a barbershop
28 By way of, for short
29 Surf's partner, on menus
30 Suffix with Smurf
31 "So it's you!"
32 Bugs Bunny or Wile E. Coyote
33 Burden to bear
34 Potato chip brand
35 Walkie-___
36 Louis Treize, Louis Quatorze and others
37 Damascus's land: Abbr.
41 Something hailed on city streets
42 Wandering
46 Camera lens setting
47 Beauty, brawn or brains
48 Land east of the Yellow Sea
49 Land west of the Yellow Sea
50 Awards for Broadway's best
51 Blood, ___ & Tears
52 Hip
53 Debussy's "Clair de ___"
54 "The Thin Man" pooch
55 What a puppy likes to do to toys and socks
56 Mongolian desert
57 Jacket fastener

by Andrea Carla Michaels

ACROSS

1 Document for foreign travel
5 Spend much time in front of the mirror
10 "Omnia vincit __" ("Love conquers all": Lat.)
14 "SportsCenter" channel
15 Rapper Kendrick
16 Designate as "commercial" or "residential," e.g.
17 Nonbinary pronoun
18 Best possible athletic performance
19 Very top
20 Figurative site of a 35-Down
23 Elevator brake inventor Elisha
24 Parched, as a desert
25 Abut
28 Close
32 Neigh : horse :: __ : sheep
33 Emerge from the ocean, say
37 French "yes"
38 Alternative to Google
40 Michael who directed "Fahrenheit 9/11"
41 Starting point for a car sale negotiation: Abbr.
42 To the back
44 Auction unit
45 Feudal superior
46 Alma mater of five U.S. presidents
47 Singers Ames and Sheeran
48 Push to do something
49 Posse
50 %: Abbr.
51 Wolf Blitzer facial feature
53 Vienna's home: Abbr.
54 Nitpick, literally
57 Old rival of MGM

58 Prefix with stasis or tarsus
60 Summa cum __
61 Tennis score after deuce
62 Sound much heard in traffic
63 Damascus's home
64 Nashville's home: Abbr.
65 Only daughter of Elizabeth II
66 Lady __, first female member of Parliament
67 French celestial being

DOWN

1 Ex-G.I.
2 "About"
3 What a volcano might do
4 Informal segue
5 Shade of blond
6 Rants and raves
7 Certain Apple
8 Half of a 1960s folk-rock group
9 Something that might be felt at a séance
10 Spring bloomer
11 Sulk
12 Last number in a countdown
13 Former secretary of state Tillerson
21 "No lie!"
22 Apple or maple
25 Alphabetically first group in the Rock & Roll Hall of Fame
26 Figurative ruler of a 35-Down
27 "Pride and Prejudice" novelist
29 Locale of many White House photo ops

30 Figurative ruler of a 35-Down
31 "Eek!"
34 Isn't oneself?
35 Feature of many a mall . . . or a place for 20-Across and 26- and 30-Down?
36 Place to make a scene?
39 Soiree, say
41 Bog down
43 Chris of "S.N.L."
45 __ job (bit of garage work)
49 Brazilian ballroom dance
52 John who wrote "No man is an island"
55 Disney's __ of Arendelle
56 Singe
59 Mimic
61 Keep __ distance

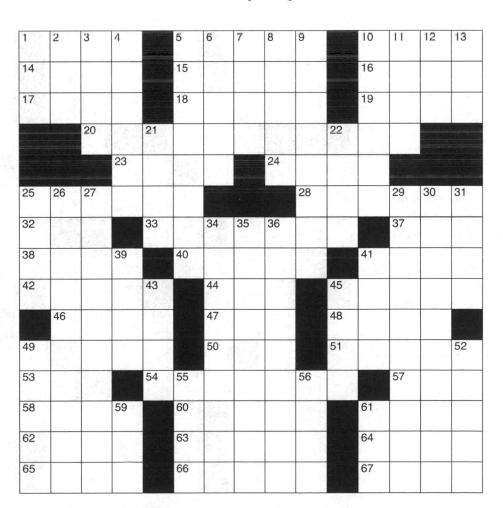

by Eric and Lori Bornstein

ACROSS

1 Surrounded by
5 Senator Mike of Idaho
10 Its state fair is much visited by politicians
14 Stream from a volcano
15 Any episode of "Parks and Recreation," now
16 Toot one's own horn
17 *Joe cool?
19 Taj Mahal locale
20 Wall Street average, with "the"
21 Backstabs
23 Annual TV awards
26 Island nation in the western Pacific
28 Opposite of yeses
29 Word before sauce or milk
30 *Amenity for jet-setters
33 Trail
35 Neither's partner
36 The first "X" of X-X-X
37 *What investigators really want to know
42 [It's c-c-old!]
43 A-to-zed lexicon, in brief
44 Attire
46 *Aromatic fragrance with a French name
51 Color TV pioneer
52 Some investments, for short
53 Untagged, in a game of tag
54 What a red-faced emoji might mean
56 Relaxing soak after a long day, maybe
58 Bay Area hub, for short
59 Fit for military service
60 Fairy tale chant from a giant . . . or the ends of the answers to the starred clues
66 Make, as money
67 Not illuminated
68 Boston's ___-Farber Cancer Institute
69 Hockey puck, e.g.
70 Animals symbolizing innocence
71 Community facility that often has a gym and pool, in brief

DOWN

1 Mahershala of "Green Book"
2 PC alternative
3 "Now ___ heard everything!"
4 Papa
5 Bird that caws
6 Official with a whistle
7 Little dog's bark
8 Southwest tribe or one of its dwellings
9 Where meaningless words go in (and out the other)
10 Letter-shaped construction support
11 Natural food producer
12 On guard against
13 Tennis great Andre
18 ___ Nostra
22 ___-frutti
23 Telepath's "gift"
24 Means of defense that doesn't actually have alligators
25 Discovery Channel program that debunked popular beliefs
26 Amateurs no more
27 Kind of reasoning
31 Red Roof ___
32 Part of a bird or museum
34 What's rounded up in a roundup
38 "The Faerie Queene" woman
39 Adroit
40 University email ending
41 Apex predator of the ocean
45 Rebuke to Marmaduke
46 Bounced back, as a sound
47 God, in the Torah
48 Quantity of stew
49 Greek goddess of wisdom
50 Peeve
55 Full of emotional swings
57 Establishment that's usually closed on Sundays
58 Poses for a photo
61 Boston's Liberty Tree, e.g.
62 Whopper junior?
63 Kin, informally
64 Tar Heels' sch.
65 Goat's bleat

by Ross Trudeau

ACROSS

1 Desktop computer covered by AppleCare
5 Opposite of buys
10 PBS science show since 1974
14 ___ Raton, Fla.
15 Clothing crease
16 Like the climate of Death Valley
17 Easy-to-peel citrus fruits
20 Sherri's twin sister on "The Simpsons"
21 Stockpile
22 Main ingredients in meringue
26 Verbal shrug
29 Warmly welcome, as a new era
30 Whack on the head
33 "Do not ___" (blackboard words)
35 Variety
36 Big name in tractors
38 Shapes of Frisbees and tiddlywinks
39 Welcome gift upon arriving at Honolulu International Airport
40 Mascara mishap
41 Sore, as after a workout
42 NASCAR champion Hamlin
44 Apt name for a car mechanic?
45 Scientist's workplace
46 Facial expressions
48 "Do you ___ my drift?"
49 What many children begin to do in kindergarten
51 Practice for a bout
53 Website with trivia quizzes
56 "Medicine" that doesn't actually contain medicine
59 Axed
60 Love to pieces
62 Estate beneficiary
63 Coffeehouse dispensers
64 First episode in a TV series
65 Change for a five
66 Try out
67 Cherry throwaways
68 World capital where the Nobel Peace Prize is awarded

DOWN

1 Creator of Watson on "Jeopardy!"
2 Protective trench
3 Target of a skin cream with Retin-A
4 Close-knit group
5 Bits of parsley
6 Man's name hidden in "reliableness"
7 Man's name hidden in "reliableness"
8 Language akin to Thai
9 Low-altitude clouds
10 Grannies
11 A.C.L.U. and others
12 Fights (for)
13 Commercials
18 Has a war of words
19 Changes, as the Constitution
23 Fritters (away), as time
24 Montana's capital
25 Peeving
26 Purple Heart, e.g.
27 TV journalist Hill
28 Crispy breakfast side dish
30 Salad base similar to Swiss chard
31 Speak from a podium, say
32 Two-time presidential candidate Ross
34 "The ___ is falling!" (Chicken Little's cry)
37 Angsty music genre
42 Worked out in a pool
43 "We should do that!"
46 Rug cleaner, informally
47 Spot for a mud facial
50 ___ & Young (accounting firm)
52 "Bless you!" elicitor
53 Closed
54 Father, in French
55 Make tweaks to
56 Dance with a king and queen
57 Actress Jessica of "Hitchcock"
58 Approximately
61 Fútbol cheer

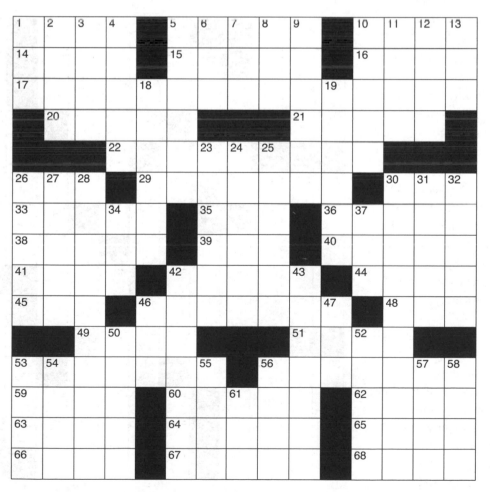

by Zhouqin Burnikel

ACROSS

1 __ Newton (cookie)
4 Salty water
9 In __ land (dreaming)
13 Many a craft brew, in brief
14 Just before the weekend
15 Big name in polo shirts
16 Alternative to Zumba
18 __ pro quo
19 "Don't get any funny __"
20 Ad __ committee
21 Opportunities to play in games
22 Govt. org. with a classified budget
24 Chevy S.U.V.
26 Donated
29 Where to order a Blizzard
34 Poem of tribute
35 Trader __ (restaurant eponym)
36 Break into with intent to steal
37 Illegally downloaded
40 Early offering, as of goods
41 More sunburned
42 Mai __ (cocktail)
43 "Look what I __!"
44 Supposed means of communication with the dead
46 Employs
47 When some local news airs
48 . . . – – . . .
50 Construction details
53 Like many HDTVs, in brief
55 Change with the times
59 Interlaced threads
60 Biggest city in South Dakota
62 Like, with "to"
63 Noted portrait photographer Anne

64 Place to apply ChapStick
65 What ice cubes do in the hot sun
66 Lock of hair
67 What the circled letters all mean

DOWN

1 Country whose name is a brand of bottled water
2 Apple tablet
3 Fixed look
4 "I'm f-f-freezing!"
5 Like the 1%
6 Nonsensical
7 Daytona 500 acronym
8 CBS logo
9 Kahlúa and Sambuca
10 Côte d'__ (French Riviera)
11 Cut of a pork roast
12 Puts two and two together, say
14 Admit, with "up"
17 Grey who wrote "Riders of the Purple Sage"
21 Chef's hat
23 Most words ending in "-ly"
25 Cars with gas/electric engines
26 Lose one's amateur status
27 Fancy goodbye
28 Giuseppe who composed "Rigoletto"
30 Assistance
31 "Holy smokes!"
32 Singer Goulding
33 Food, water and air
38 Next (to)
39 Things milking machines attach to

40 Number on a miniature golf card
42 Some reading for an I.R.S. auditor
45 Slicker
46 Meat-inspecting org.
49 Ham-handed sorts
50 Participated in the first third of a triathlon
51 Rude touch
52 "Don't be __" (Google motto)
54 Clothing, informally
56 Friend in a conflict
57 Ballet bend
58 Measures of salt and sugar: Abbr.
60 One crying "Hup, two, three, four!": Abbr.
61 Critical marks on treasure maps

by Wren Schultz

ACROSS

1 Library catalog listing after "author"
6 Ribbit : frog :: ___ : cat
10 Bit of land in the sea: Sp.
14 Author Asimov
15 Scrabble or Boggle
16 Challenging vegetables to eat with a fork
17 Harmonica
19 ___ and sciences
20 What "Yes, I'm willing!" signifies
21 Contend
22 Talks effusively
25 Place to get some barbecue
28 It might be confused with a termite
29 Tanning lotion fig.
31 Pointy-leaved desert plants
32 Lo-o-ong bath
34 ___ Asia (China, Japan and environs)
37 Poor grades
38 Dummy
41 Bog fuel
42 Brontë's "Jane ___"
43 Quick bite to eat
46 Tranquil
48 Grp. overseeing the World Series
50 Wildebeest
51 Negative repercussions
54 Individual
56 Capital of Georgia: Abbr.
57 "You don't have to take responsibility for the mistake"
59 Tidy
61 Stand-in during a film shoot . . . or a hint to 17-, 25-, 38- and 51-Across
65 Platform for a ceremony
66 Send off, as rays
67 Autumn bloom
68 Follower of hop and skip
69 "The lady ___ protest too much": "Hamlet"
70 More recent

DOWN

1 Dickens's Tiny ___
2 Prefix with -therm
3 Letter after sigma
4 Gate closer
5 Sounds heard in canyons
6 People in charge: Abbr.
7 Raring to go
8 Neighbor of a Saudi and Yemeni
9 Passed
10 Brewery letters
11 Ones leading the blind, maybe
12 Jennifer Lopez and Christina Aguilera, for two
13 Good things to have
18 Without assurance of purchase
22 Word after laughing or natural
23 Half of dos
24 Assert one's ownership, as to land
26 "Hey ___" (Beatles hit)
27 Roughly 71% of the earth's surface
30 Like many Rolex watches sold on the street
33 Natural ability
35 Apt letters missing from "_tea_th_"
36 Six years, for a U.S. senator
39 Electricity or water, e.g.: Abbr.
40 Assisted
41 Level off at a higher point
44 ___ Balls (chocolaty snack)
45 Attila the ___
46 Three-ingredient lunchbox staple, familiarly
47 Lightly touched, as with a handkerchief
49 Express sorrow over
52 Sports replay effect
53 Lost patience
55 Do something else with
58 George Washington's chopping down a cherry tree, e.g.
60 Small recipe amt.
62 "As an aside," in a text
63 Film director Spike
64 Flub

by Adrienne Atkins

ACROSS

1 —-schmancy
6 Apple's digital assistant
10 Sandwiches that may use Skippy and Smuckers, informally
14 Regions
15 The "Odyssey," for one
16 __ Canal, connector of the Hudson River to the Great Lakes
17 Arkansas's capital
19 "__ from New York, it's . . ."
20 Bonny young woman
21 Overhaul
22 "Superbad" co-star Seth
23 Loss offsetter
25 Derrière
26 Bicolor cookies also called half-moons
32 Hold responsible
33 Cause of some nose-wrinkling
34 "How was __ know?"
35 Red, as a steak
36 Portmanteau for denim cutoffs
38 Condition treated by Adderall, for short
39 Corp. giant spelled backward inside "giant"
40 Something tried out for in a tryout
41 Follows, as orders
42 Final practice before the big show
46 Opening between mountains
47 Opening for a coin
48 One of a pair of a carnival entertainer
50 How many times the Washington Nationals have won the World Series
52 Chocolate candy with a caramel center
56 Rice-shaped pasta
57 Fashion designer associated with the item spelled out by the starts of 17-, 26- and 42-Across

59 Clown of renown
60 Prerevolution Russian leader
61 Had a role to play
62 Obsessive fan, in slang
63 Plane assignment
64 Feed, as a fire

DOWN

1 Leaf-changing season
2 Prima donna's big moment
3 Brooklyn basketball team
4 Tie in tic-tac-toe
5 Big inits. in fashion
6 Tennis star Williams
7 Cher holder?
8 Puerto __
9 "Gross!"
10 House speaker Nancy
11 Flash of genius
12 "__ Talkin'," #1 hit for the Bee Gees
13 Observed
18 Composer Satie
22 German industrial valley
24 There's only one spot for this
25 Deuces
26 Former British P.M. Tony
27 Circular food item that may come in a 16" square box
28 Up, on a compass
29 Banned pesticide, for short
30 __ alcohol (fuel source)
31 Installs, as a lawn
32 __ Rutter, "Jeopardy!" contestant with the all-time highest winnings ($4.9+ million)
36 Places for tips

37 Valuable deposit
38 Existing in the mind only
40 "Hey, over here!"
41 Spanish gold
43 Place for a brawl in a western
44 Accompany on the red carpet, say
45 One of the Baldwin brothers
48 Bawls
49 Horse's gait
50 Slowly seep (out)
51 Org. with bowl games
53 "Hold __ your hat!"
54 Vegetable paired with potato in a soup
55 Quaint shoppe descriptor
57 Adds to an email chain, in a way
58 Possesses

by Michael Lieberman

ACROSS

1 Come ___ with (accompany)
6 Cover for a smartphone
10 Lines at the cash register, for short?
14 ___ Day (September observance)
15 Vizio or Panasonic product
16 Snow clearer
17 Sleuth for hire
19 ___ chips (Hawaiian snack)
20 Poem of praise
21 Angel's instrument
22 Entrance hall
23 Perform an act of kindness, in a way
26 Kind of seeds on a bagel
29 Musk of SpaceX
30 Actor Wilson of "Wedding Crashers"
31 ___ Peninsula, area above Singapore
33 Gorilla
36 1977 #1 Eagles hit
40 Gives the go-ahead
41 Desi of "I Love Lucy"
42 George Washington bills
43 Popular berry
44 What loves company, in a saying
46 It might catch a thief or a speeder
51 President after Washington
52 Library item
53 Dance style for Bill Robinson or Gregory Hines
56 Jeans maker Strauss
57 Be willing to accept whatever . . . or a hint to the ends of 17-, 23-, 36- and 46-Across
60 Bear's retreat
61 Skating leap
62 Crunchy, colorful commercial candies
63 Otherwise
64 Bloody
65 Stuck (to)

DOWN

1 Brand for Rover
2 Cooking grease
3 Annual drama award
4 Election mo.
5 Kind of cracker needed for a proper s'more
6 Paris sweetheart
7 Thoroughly proficient
8 Mudhole
9 Garden of Eden woman
10 Train direction from Manhattan to the Bronx
11 Spanish beach
12 Tool for preparing apples
13 Weapon in a scabbard
18 Actor Diggs
22 Cold treat with a rhyming name
23 Window square
24 "___ Navidad"
25 Snowman in "Frozen"
26 London theater district
27 Furry "Star Wars" creature
28 6-1, 4-6 and 7-6, in tennis
31 Frenzied
32 Montgomery's state: Abbr.
33 Hathaway of "The Devil Wears Prada"
34 Where boats tie up
35 "Piece of cake!"
37 Shoestrings
38 Commercial lead-in to Apple
39 Parks of Montgomery
43 Idolize, say
44 ___ Mix, brand for Whiskers
45 Bothering
46 Popular Berry
47 Perfect
48 Tennis's ___ Cup
49 More up to the task
50 "Good Golly, Miss ___"
53 Kind of traffic, familiarly
54 Helper
55 Possible condition for a war vet, for short
57 Cloth for cleaning
58 Kitchen utensil brand
59 Abbr. on a business card

by Erika Ettin

ACROSS

1 Fills with wonderment
5 Rating for "Supergirl" or "Gilmore Girls"
9 Piece of the pie
14 The __ of one's existence
15 Get wind of
16 Prop for a painter
17 Abbr. for routing of mail
18 Spooky-sounding lake?
19 Format for old computer games
20 Food for Little Miss Muffet
23 "__ the Force, Luke"
24 Drink in a tavern
25 Increases, as the pot
29 __ Madre (Western range)
31 Chinese dissident artist
33 Like Shakespeare's feet?
35 Common injury locale for an athlete, in brief
36 U.S. Naval Academy anthem
41 Lyric poem
42 Pacific weather phenomenon
43 Neighbor of Botswana
47 Driver's license, e.g., in brief
51 Grab 40 winks
52 Music genre for Weezer or Fall Out Boy
53 Follower of Red or Dead
54 Breakup song by Fleetwood Mac
58 Energy alternative to wind
61 Shoelace annoyance
62 Snooty manners
63 In the loop
64 Tilt-a-Whirl, e.g.
65 Get ready, as for surgery
66 Messages that may include emojis
67 x and y, on a graph
68 "M*A*S*H" co-star Alan

DOWN

1 Something you can always count on
2 1960s dance craze
3 Main dish
4 Email button
5 1836 site to "remember"
6 Science fiction pioneer Jules
7 Stamp on an invoice
8 Increased, as the pot
9 Withdraw formally
10 Mom of Princes William and Harry
11 Home of Tel Aviv: Abbr.
12 Bigwig hired by a board
13 Street frequented by Freddy Krueger
21 Actress __ Jessica Parker
22 Hem and __
26 Freebies at a corporate event
27 Field for many Silicon Valley jobs
28 Shipment from Alaska's North Slope
30 Rocker Ocasek of the Cars
31 What a bride walks down
32 The Who's "__ See for Miles"
34 Batch of beer
36 Tennis score after deuce
37 6-Down's submarine captain
38 Nintendo controllers
39 Fund, as a fellowship
40 Org. with Summer and Winter Games
41 Parts of lbs.
44 Bergman's "Casablanca" co-star
45 Islands west of Lisbon
46 Queen __ (pop nickname)
48 Eddying
49 Stood on its hind legs, as a horse
50 Place to be pampered
52 Wear down bit by bit
55 Southern soup ingredient
56 Operating system developed at Bell Labs
57 California vineyard valley
58 Took a rest . . . or a test?
59 Be in debt
60 Not strict

by Andrea Carla Michaels and Doug Peterson

ACROSS

1 Make sense
6 Many a get-rich-quick scheme
10 Meal cooked in a Crock-Pot
14 Atlanta train system
15 Wife of Zeus
16 Domesticated
17 Moolah
18 Distance between belt holes, maybe
19 Sign at a highway interchange
20 Capable of floating, as a balloon
23 Low-ranking "Star Trek" officer: Abbr.
24 Sombrero, e.g.
25 Smidgen
26 Neon or xenon
27 Soul singer Thomas
29 Wail
32 Sanctimonious
36 Ken, to Barbie
37 "Rocks," in a drink
38 Captain's place on a ship
39 Imposing and then some
44 Units on a football field: Abbr.
45 ___ Susan (dining table centerpiece)
46 How long it might take for a mountain to form
47 Word before "bite" or "go"
48 Rapper ___-Z
49 Word sometimes confused with "lie"
52 "Let's put things in perspective" . . . or a title for this puzzle
57 Martin Luther King's "Letter From Birmingham ___"
58 Debtors' notes
59 Brain divisions
60 Gawk at

61 ___ menu (where to find Cut, Copy and Paste)
62 Longtime Yankees manager Joe
63 Runner Usain
64 Where bears hibernate
65 Gives a thumbs-up

DOWN

1 Saunter
2 1950s–'60s singer Bobby
3 Bottom of the barrel
4 Salt Lake City's home
5 Stir-fried noodle dish
6 Jersey
7 Penny
8 Feature over many a doorway
9 Honorific for Gandhi
10 Ending with farm or home
11 Move from the gate to the runway, say
12 Mideast bigwig
13 "Caution—___ paint" (sign)
21 Simplicity
22 Vindaloo accompaniment
26 When repeated, water cooler sound
27 Like a poison ivy rash
28 Mother of Zeus (and an anagram of 15-Across)
29 "Give my compliments to the ___"
30 Part to play
31 "De-e-elish!"
32 Chairperson, e.g.
33 Cousins of paddles
34 Cracker brand with a yellow-and-blue logo
35 Like Girl Scout "Mints"
36 Pioneering journalist Nellie
40 Woman's name that's also a Spanish pronoun
41 Made a comeback
42 1963 Best Actress Patricia
43 Never betraying
47 Speck of land in the sea
48 Kids around
49 The Scales
50 Big office supply brand
51 Positive responses
52 Shakespeare villain who says "Virtue? A fig!"
53 Cash register drawer
54 Rich vein of ore
55 Pompeii or Machu Picchu
56 Nabbed
57 What you're hired to do

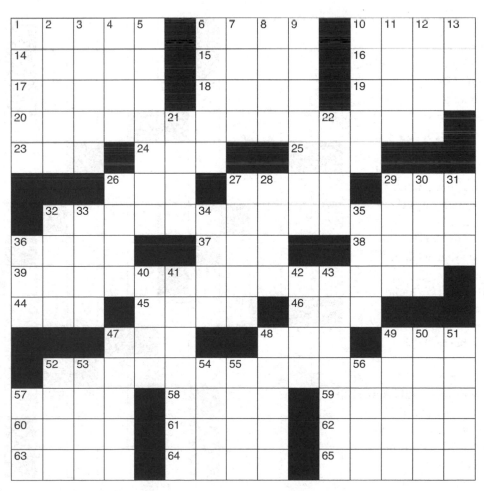

by Jacob Stulberg

ACROSS

1 Potato, informally
5 Desert succulent
10 Net material
14 . . . approximately
15 __ Heights (Syria/Israel border area)
16 Reverberation
17 "So, this red thing, Mom? This is not good."
19 Ending with church or party
20 Wild time at the mall
21 Assesses visually
23 Lounge around
26 Amend a tax return, perhaps
27 "The French one is my favorite. Wait, no, the pretzel one."
32 Lamb's mother
33 Gaze intently
34 Get out of __ (leave town)
38 Boring
40 Mexican marinade made with chili pepper
42 Sonnet or ode
43 Request from
45 Blissful spots
47 Printer malfunction
48 "Eww, mollusks . . . I don't know, didn't this make me sick last time?"
51 Actress Meryl with nine Golden Globe Awards
54 "Buona __" (Italian greeting)
55 Render impossible
58 Fumble (for)
62 It's a crime to lie under it
63 "Wow, Mom, this is like at a restaurant! Dibs on the chocolate pudding!"
66 Garfield's canine pal
67 Energy giant synonymous with corporate scandal
68 "I get it now"
69 Ecosystem built by corals
70 Seat at a counter
71 Has an evening meal

DOWN

1 Weeps loudly
2 Get ready for a test, say
3 __ name and password
4 "Ooh, spill the tea!"
5 "__ before beauty"
6 Republicans, for short
7 __ vera
8 Change into different forms
9 Walks in
10 Epic failure
11 Culprit in some food poisoning cases
12 Conch, e.g.
13 Animal in a stable
18 Rises up on its hind legs, as a 13-Down
22 Item strung on a necklace
24 Actress Catherine __-Jones
25 Manages to elude
27 Singer McEntire
28 You can't say they won't give a hoot!
29 Reveal, as confidential information
30 Gradually wear away, as soil
31 Rises up in protest
35 Training place for martial arts
36 One of 10 on a 10-speed
37 Award won multiple times by "Modern Family" and "All in the Family"
39 Popular meal kit company (or the mother of the food critic featured in this puzzle?)
41 "You can count __"
44 Gas or coal
46 Twilled fabric for suits
49 Sea foams
50 Former Philippine president Ferdinand
51 Scent of an animal
52 Exchange
53 Fix, as a knot
56 Journey's "__ Stop Believin'"
57 Continental currency
59 Honolulu's home
60 Sound of sitting down heavily
61 Fraternal order
64 Phillipa __, Tony nominee for "Hamilton"
65 NBC sketch show, in brief

by Pamela F. Davis

ACROSS

1 Negative media coverage, in brief
6 Undergraduate's declaration
11 Consumer protection org.
14 Open-air rooms
15 Olio di __ (bread dip at a trattoria)
16 Water: Fr.
17 Marine inhabitant that's an animal, not a plant, despite what it's called
19 __ de Triomphe
20 Tiny drink
21 Org. with missions to Mars
22 Put back in the suitcase
24 43,560 square feet
26 Nightclub
27 Angry shout to a miscreant
29 Prince who married Meghan Markle
32 Swollen mark
33 Garden tool with a long handle
34 Heed
35 Top Olympic prizes
37 Many a sacrifice play in baseball
38 Padre's sister
39 Make do
40 Bar mitzvah reading
41 Sobriquet for Simón Bolívar
45 Actress Lohan of "Mean Girls"
46 Camrys and Corollas
50 Challenges for dry cleaners
51 Ares and Apollo, to Zeus
52 Insect that can carry up to 50 times its body weight
53 "Ready, __, fire!"
54 Observation satellite
57 Service charge
58 Fictional detective Nero
59 Wide receiver __ Beckham Jr.
60 Shape on a winding road
61 Peeved states
62 Blender setting

DOWN

1 Low opera voice
2 Had a home-cooked meal
3 Curtain
4 Snapchat transmission, for short
5 Vulgar, as some humor
6 Dull brown, as hair
7 __ mater
8 Triangular sail
9 Attire for the Mario Bros. or the Minions
10 Cheese-on-toast dish
11 Co-star of TV's "Maude"
12 Only Spanish city to host the Olympics
13 Facial feature of Disney's Goofy
18 Actor Elwes
23 Butter unit
25 Out of kilter
26 Fed a line to
28 What can barely give a hoot?
29 Place to store valuables when traveling
30 Skills
31 Shawn Carter for Jay-Z and Tracy Morrow for Ice-T
35 Be lenient with
36 Grand Ole __
37 The Bronx or Brooklyn, informally
39 Employer of Norah O'Donnell
40 Place to buy gifts for kids
42 Ugandan tyrant __ Amin
43 Makes amends (for)
44 "__ mention it!"
47 Electrified weapon
48 What a maxi dress reaches
49 Fashion
51 De-clump, as flour
55 Yale collegian
56 Yale URL ender

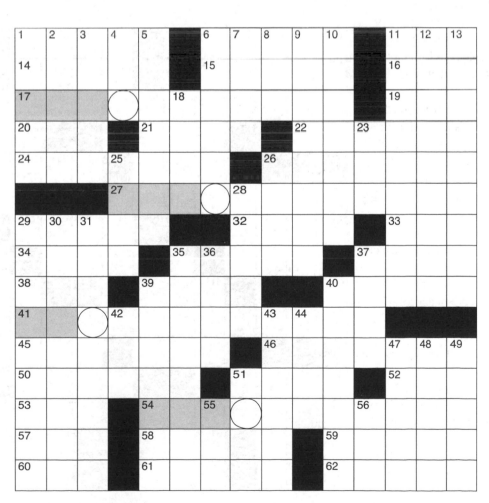

by Peter Gordon

ACROSS

1 Hard to understand
7 Vegan protein source
11 Electric guitarist's need
14 It makes an auto shine
15 Spirited horse
16 Luau finger food
17 Song lyric before "short and stout"
20 Turn down, as lights
21 "Check this out!"
22 Out of practice
23 "The Simpsons" character voiced by Nancy Cartwright
24 ___ to the throne
26 Attorney general under George W. Bush
33 Sully
34 1960s Ron Howard TV role
35 Eggs in a fertility lab
36 End of a cigarette or rifle
37 Were in accord
39 Nephew of Donald Duck
40 Number that never goes down
41 Morrison who said "A writer's life and work are not a gift to mankind; they are its necessity"
42 Some pork cuts
43 Appeasing, idiomatically
47 Writes
48 Gape
49 What designated drivers should be
52 Taurus symbol
53 Give silent approval
56 Grilled Japanese dish on skewers
60 What a dipstick measures the level of
61 Prep for publication
62 Where this puzzle's circled letters can be found
63 Part of the body that's stubbed
64 Trick
65 ___ network

DOWN

1 The "A" of DNA
2 Oscar-winning Malek
3 Do some last-minute studying
4 Leatherworker's pointed tool
5 Fancy work from a manicurist
6 Squeeze money from
7 Format of much AM radio
8 Metal in a mine
9 What Jack Sprat couldn't eat, in a nursery rhyme
10 Transform using mobile technology, as a market
11 TikTok and Zoom, for two
12 Not worth debating
13 Feel sorry for
18 Band with the 1983 #1 hit "62-Across"
19 Surrounding glow
23 Like the wire in paper clips
24 "Cross my heart and ___ to die"
25 Oklahoma city
26 Facing the pitcher
27 Ha-ha
28 Dog to avoid
29 Pull out all the stops
30 Nephew of Donald Duck
31 100- or 200-meter, e.g.
32 Final authority
37 Enlist
38 Quaint lodgings
39 Sound of a car or goose
41 Brought up the rear?
42 Disreputable sort
44 International grp. with a 1970s U.S. embargo
45 Water: Sp.
46 Southeast Europe's ___ Peninsula
49 Person who may speak with a brogue
50 Home of Cincinnati
51 Ill humor
52 Unit that may be preceded by kilo-, mega- or giga-
53 Black: Fr.
54 Killer whale
55 Telephone
57 Univ. URL ending
58 ___ in the bud
59 ___TV (cable channel with "Impractical Jokers")

by Kevin Christian

1

```
S A M O A . . A B S . S I G H
A L A R M B E L L S . O T R O
G A S S T A T I O N . S H E A
A S T O . C A B O . B O O E R
. . . S O L I D G R O U N D .
I M D O W N . . . L A N G . .
M A R D I . O L M E C . H O P
P L A S M A S C R E E N T V S
S I M . S T U D S . L O S E S
. . A G U A . . . R E T O R T
L I Q U I D A S S E T . . . .
A D U L T . Q U I P . O N I T
N O E L . J U S T A P H A S E
A L E E . D A I S Y C H A I N
I S N T . S S E . P I N T S .
```

2

```
C U B A . . B O A S . . H A M
A H A B . H O R D E . C O L A
R O B E . O R G A N D O N O R
S H Y . M U G . G A R R E T S
. . B A R N . T I T A N . . .
F L O R I D A R O O M . G M T
R A N G . S R O . R A H R A H
O W N U P . F I G . S U E D E
S N E E R S . K I A . N E R F
H S T . A T L A S R O C K E T
. . C Y R U S . M O H S . . .
C I C A D A S . D O H . A R K
L O C K O F H A I R . C L U E
A N N E . E L W A Y . E A S Y
P S Y . D Y E S . . O D E S .
```

3

```
W O O S . P A L S . A D L I B
A U N T . A V O W . A I O L I
L I E U . W A V E S H E L L O
L O A F S . I D E S T . . . .
S U R F T H E N E T . S E L F
T I M . R A Y . . T O N E R .
. . P O L E S . S A D D A Y .
. S H E L L S O U T C A S H .
B E E T L E . S N I T S . . .
T A R T S . U R I . B A E . .
U S E R . P A L M S C A R D S
. . I S D U E . S C O O P . .
B E A C H F R O N T . H O R A
L A T K E . A N E W . O M E N
T R E S S . S E G O . O S S A
```

4

```
S N I T . B O O R . G E S S O
W I N E . A N T E . A G A I N
E X T E N S I O N . B O R N E
D E O . E S T H E R . C A P .
E D W A R D . E X C L A I M .
. . N O R T H . S H E S . . .
P A S T . U R I S . I N T W O
E X C O M M U N I C A T I O N
R E U N E . E T C H . I C E S
. . L I S T . S K I L L . . .
E X P O S E S . C O S M O S .
P E T . A L A S K A . A R I .
I N U S E . E X P E N D I N G
C O R E R . E L A N . A N O N
S N E E R . K E Y S . B E T S
```

5

```
D I S . C D R O M . A B Y S S
A R E . A R O M A . L O O P Y
T I L . R O D E S H O T G U N
A S L E E P . N A O H . A R C
. . B E T S Y . D U A L . . .
A L Y R A I S M A N . M B A S
L A D . K N E E . D I A L I N
I N A N E . R R S . N O O S E
A C T O R S . G O O D . O L E
S E E D . W H E Y P O W D E R
. . E R I E . A U N T Y . . .
U S B . A N A L . L E S M I Z
C H A N G E L A N E S . A K A
L U N G E . E V E N I . R E C
A N D O R . R A S T A . Y A K
```

6

```
L I P . M A T T E R . V A V A
A V A . E R R A T A . E R I N
M A R B L E A R C H . N E R D
A N T E . A C S . L I N E R .
. . H A W . T I C T A C T O E
A G E L E S S . R A G E . . .
H O N E S T . D E L A . S O B
O N O . T A R H E E L . E P A
Y E N . B I E L . S A S S E S
. . L A R D . S E X T A L K .
L E M O N S O L E . Y A M . .
A B A C K . I C E . F E T A .
W O R K . A B O U T A F O O T
N O D E . C O N R A D . I R A
S K I T . E A S E L S . L I D
```

7

W	A	S	P		R	E	S	T	S			G	N	P
O	P	I	E		A	L	L	O	W		F	U	E	L
R	I	F	E		D	I	A	N	A		E	N	V	Y
D	E	T	R	O	I	T	T	I	G	E	R	S		
I	C	E		D	O	E				A	M	I	S	S
S	E	R	V	E			S	I	T	T	I	G	H	T
		I	L	K		E	C	O		H	E	Y		
	S	P	L	I	T	T	I	C	K	E	T			
O	W	L		W	I	T		K	E	G				
W	A	I	T	T	I	M	E		I	O	T	A	S	
E	D	G	E	D			S	A	T		R	N	A	
	H	A	S	I	T	B	O	T	H	W	A	Y	S	
B	O	T	S		S	H	I	L	L		I	D	O	S
F	R	E	E		L	A	R	V	A		R	E	N	O
F	E	D			A	I	D	E	S		E	D	E	N

8

S	O	L	O	S		K	E	E	N		E	M	I	T
A	L	I	C	E		O	R	C	A		M	A	M	A
F	I	G	H	T	N	I	G	H	T		U	R	N	S
E	V	E	R	S	O		O	O	H		D	O	T	
R	A	R	E		A	T	E		E	V	I	T	E	
			W	H	I	T	E	K	N	I	G	H	T	
B	O	T	C	H		N	A	M	E		B	R	E	E
U	P	R	O	O	T	S		E	N	D	E	A	R	S
B	E	A	N		N	E	A	R		A	S	S	E	T
B	R	I	G	H	T	L	I	G	H	T				
L	A	N	A	I		L	E	I		F	E	E	L	
E	T	S		P	A	T		K	A	R	A	T	E	
T	O	T	E		Q	U	I	T	E	R	I	G	H	T
E	R	O	S		U	G	L	I		A	T	E	A	M
A	S	P	S		A	S	K	S		B	O	R	N	E

9

V	E	R	D	I		A	S	A	P		J	O	A	N
A	D	O	R	N		M	E	M	O		U	N	T	O
L	U	A	U	S		P	R	O	P	A	G	A	T	E
		D	I	E	T		U	S	E	R		P	I	X
C	A	R	D	A	M	O	M		A	T	A	R	I	
A	T	A		M	I	R		C	A	B	A	R	E	T
B	O	G	S		C	L	E	R	I	C				
	M	E	T	A	P	H	Y	S	I	C	I	A	N	
		E	D	D	I	E	S		T	B	A	R		
C	R	A	W	D	A	D		N	A	S		U	M	A
H	O	R	S	E		C	A	S	T	A	N	E	T	
A	T	E		R	I	G	A		K	I	N	D		
P	A	N	A	S	O	N	I	C		G	N	A	T	S
E	T	A	L		T	A	R	A		M	I	N	O	R
L	E	S	T		A	W	O	L		A	E	T	N	A

10

P	I	N		P	A	T	E	N	T		F	D	I	C
E	S	E		O	L	I	V	E	R		T	E	R	I
R	A	W	F	O	O	T	A	G	E		M	B	A	S
P	I	E	R	R	E		A	S	P	E	R			
S	A	R	I		M	I	T		R	A	I	M	I	
H	A	L	F	B	A	K	E	D	I	D	E	A	S	
			L	I	E	G	E		W	O	E	F	U	L
A	N	G		T	M	I		H	E	R		S	I	A
C	O	R	O	N	A		P	O	E	T	S			
C	O	O	K	E	D	T	H	E	B	O	O	K	S	
T	R	U	S	S		E	D	S		D	I	C	E	
		P	I	S	A	N		S	O	O	T	H	E	
P	R	I	G		B	U	R	N	T	U	M	B	E	R
E	D	E	N		B	R	E	Y	E	R		A	M	I
P	A	S	S		R	E	N	E	W	S		G	E	E

11

B	E	S	T		F	R	A	N		B	A	N	A	L
A	V	E	R		L	E	G	O		A	L	I	B	I
B	A	R	(I)	T	O	N	E	S		N	(A)	C	H	O
E	N	(V)		(O)	W	E		E	T	D		(H)	O	N
	(E)	L	L	E		B	R	O	I	(L)	E	R	S	
R	A	T	E	D	R		A	(I)	N	T	I			
A	M	(I)	T	Y		B	I	N	G		A	C	D	C
M	M	M		A	M	A	L	G	A	M		R	U	E
P	O	E	T		A	L	E	S		A	M	I	N	O
		A	C	(I)	D	Y		G	R	A	T	E	S	
E	N	D	(Z)	O	N	E	S		A	G	R	I		
K	I	A		(A)	S	A		B	R	O		(C)	O	E
E	V	I	(L)	S		G	O	O	D	(T)	H	I	N	G
B	E	R	E	(T)		L	A	N	E		(I)	S	T	O
Y	A	Y	A	S		E	T	O	N		D	M	V	S

12

B	U	S	H		C	A	I	R	O			S	A	M
A	N	T	E		A	L	D	E	R		W	I	N	E
S	T	O	R	M	C	L	O	U	D		A	R	T	S
A	I	R	D	A	T	E		P	E	E	V	I	S	H
L	E	E		R	U	N	S		R	A	Y			
			L	A	S		O	V	E	R	L	O	A	D
C	I	V	I	C		S	A	I	D		I	D	L	E
O	M	E	G	A		C	N	N		S	N	I	P	E
M	A	T	H		F	A	D	E		T	E	N	O	R
E	M	O	T	I	O	N	S		S	O	S			
		B	A	R		O	P	E	L		G	A	P	
L	E	G	U	M	E	S		E	P	I	T	O	M	E
O	V	A	L		S	W	E	A	T	D	R	O	P	S
L	I	M	B		E	A	R	L	E		O	S	L	O
A	L	E		E	G	R	E	T		T	E	E	S	

13

W	A	S			I	H	O	P	E			S	T	A	T	S
A	L	L			M	O	D	E	L			E	R	N	I	E
S	O	Y		C	O	D	E	B	R	E	A	K	E	R		
P	E	A	P	O	D		R	A	E			S	L	I	T	
		S	E	L	L	S			A	T	H	E	N	A		
S	T	A	N	D	U	P	C	O	M	I	C					
C	A	F			M	A	R	X		C	A	B	I	N		
A	R	O	M	A		C	E	L		K	N	I	F	E		
N	E	X	U	S		E	D	I	T			T	S	A		
		C	H	I	R	O	P	R	A	C	T	O	R			
D	A	S	H	E	S			S	A	D	I	E				
I	D	E	A		L	A	S			I	A	G	R	E	E	
G	E	T	C	R	A	C	K	I	N	G		E	V	A		
A	L	O	H	A		T	E	P	E	E		N	E	S		
T	E	N	O	N		S	E	A	R	S		D	R	Y		

14

S	A	C	K		J	E	E	R		S	C	R	U	B
H	E	H	E		O	G	L	E		C	A	U	S	E
A	S	I	N		I	A	M	B		U	R	B	A	N
G	O	L	D	E	N	D	O	O	D	L	E			
S	P	E	A	K			R	U	P	E	E	S		
		L	E	A	V	E	N	O	T	R	A	C	E	
M	E	W	L		G	I	N			E	S	S	A	Y
U	M	A		C	O	D	D	L	E	D		E	R	E
F	A	I	R	Y			E	A	R		S	L	E	D
F	I	V	E	C	A	R	D	D	R	A	W			
	L	E	S	L	I	E				S	E	A	M	S
		C	O	M	E	D	Y	S	K	E	T	C	H	
T	R	A	I	N		F	E	A	T		T	A	R	O
W	A	Y	N	E		E	M	M	A		E	R	I	E
O	P	E	D	S		R	O	S	Y		N	I	B	S

15

P	A	W		R	O	A	M	S			G	E	A	R
U	S	A		E	N	T	O	M	B		O	L	G	A
P	A	L	L	B	E	A	R	E	R		E	L	O	N
I	D	E	A	S			E	L	A	P	S	E		
L	A	S	S		P	E	L	L	G	R	A	N	T	
			I	R	A	N		S	H	O	P	P	E	R
C	O	C	K	A	P	O	O			N	E	A	T	O
A	N	O		P	I	L	L	B	U	G		G	O	O
S	T	R	I	P			E	A	S	E	M	E	N	T
H	A	P	L	E	S	S		L	E	D	E			
	P	O	L	L	T	A	K	E	R		T	O	T	E
	R	E	S	O	L	E			M	O	T	H	S	
S	W	A	G		P	U	L	L	Q	U	O	T	E	S
I	O	T	A		S	T	P	A	U	L		E	R	A
P	E	E	L			E	S	T	E	E		R	E	Y

16

F	A	K	E	D		B	B	C			D	E	C	A	F
I	C	I	E	R		L	E	O			O	R	A	T	E
J	E	L	L	Y	R	O	L	L			G	A	M	E	R
I	D	O			O	B	I	T			S	T	E	I	N
			H	O	U	S	E	S	I	T		R	N	S	
A	S	S	O	R	T				N	A	D	A			
R	E	P	R	O		P	U	B	C	R	A	W	L		
T	A	R	A		A	T	R	I	A		M	O	O	D	
	M	I	C	S	T	A	N	D		L	A	R	V	A	
		N	E	A	T				R	I	S	K	E	D	
E	G	G		C	A	K	E	W	A	L	K				
N	O	T	C	H		E	L	E	C			W	O	E	
A	F	I	R	E		B	A	B	Y	S	T	E	P	S	
C	A	D	E	T		A	T	M		P	O	P	U	P	
T	R	E	E	S		B	E	D		A	N	T	S	Y	

17

C	L	A	W		S	C	A	B		C	H	R	I	S
H	A	Z	E		O	H	N	O		P	E	A	R	L
O	P	A	L		D	I	D	G	E	R	I	D	O	O
I	T	L	L	D	O		Y	O	N		D	I	N	G
R	O	E		U	M	P		T	A	P	I	O	C	A
S	P	A	D	E		O	B	A	M	A		I	A	N
		O	S	A	K	A		O	R	I	N	G	S	
	M	I	D	O	C	E	A	N	R	I	D	G	E	
E	A	T	O	U	T		E	A	S	E	L			
A	L	S		T	R	A	D	E		T	E	M	P	E
S	L	A	S	H	E	R		S	K	A		A	I	R
T	O	G	A		S	A	D		U	L	S	T	E	R
B	R	I	D	E	S	M	A	I	D		E	Z	R	A
A	C	R	I	D		I	N	D	O		W	O	R	N
Y	A	L	E	U		S	A	S	S		S	H	E	D

18

H	A	T	H		B	A	H		O	T	T	A	W	A
E	R	O	O		A	R	T		S	A	U	N	A	S
M	A	R	C		T	I	M	H	O	R	T	O	N	S
	B	A	K	E	S	A	L	E				D	D	E
S	H	E	L				B	O	X	S	E	A	T	
		Y	E	A	T	S		C	I	A				
S	C	E	N	A	R	I	O		A	N	Y	O	N	E
H	O	P	I		C	O	L	A	S		I	V	A	N
E	N	I	G	M	A		A	L	I	E	N	A	T	E
			H	E	N		R	E	O	R	G			
S	T	U	T	T	E	R				I	S	S	A	
U	R	N			A	P	R	I	C	O	T	S		
M	A	P	L	E	S	Y	R	U	P		R	E	P	O
A	L	I	G	N	S		E	T	A		R	A	I	N
C	A	N	A	D	A		P	H	D		Y	M	C	A

19

```
MEMO  INCA  PESTS
OPEC  DEAL  EXPAT
WENTDOWNTHETUBE
SENOR STOOL ROE
   OPUS   POSTOP
CANIGETALIFT
OBI SLICE FATED
METZ FLEAS NAPA
BLEAK LISTS XIS
   PASSTHETORCH
COPSTO   MOUE
OHO ROBOT IGLOO
CASHINONESCHIPS
ORION ACRE TEES
AETNA TEMP AFRO
```

20

```
ABBA ABLY   GAP
CARL FRIED NABS
CLUE LAMAR OTAY
ELLEMACPHERSON
SEE ACE  WEIRDS
STEED SANDRAOH
 RAT ICE  DNA
 SAMANTHABEE
REP NEO ROO
KAYHAGAN ASSAM
ORNATE ABS HUE
 WOMENOFLETTERS
DIVA TROVE OHOH
AGES SERIF MERE
YSL  SANS BRAD
```

21

```
BLATHER   PLAZA
ARCHIVAL SAILOR
HOMEPAGE CLEARS
ANEW MUMBOJUMBO
 ETA OOO  BAN
JIBBERJABBER
IRE LIEN YEARN
BAAS EDGER FLOE
EQUAL EVEN TLC
 GOBBLEDYGOOK
AHA VIA CUB
BALDERDASH SEAM
USERID EPIPHANY
TOXINS RANSACKS
SNAPS  SAYWHAT
```

22

```
SPAS PEACH STUD
EACH EMCEE AONE
NAME ATARI SPIN
TREBEK BIGSHOTS
 CARPS SHEAF
CHO GEE ETA TBA
HERR RAD ORWHAT
RIPE FLUFF AERO
IDOIDO GIF XMEN
SIR ORC DAN ODE
 AROMA OSCAR
INTERACT HORNED
RAIN NAOMI TIVO
KNOT COMBO ONEG
SONS ESSEN OGRE
```

23

```
LASTS TEXAS SPA
ALEUT ALERT AUK
DIANAPRINCE FBI
DELAYED ASPHALT
ENE EYE ARIA
REVAMP DCCOMICS
SEEME TUPAC
 LYNDACARTER
 SARAS AVOID
GALGADOT CLAUSE
AQUA EBB TOT
LUMBAGO LETMEBE
LIP WONDERWOMAN
OLE LULUS OVERT
PAD STYES SENSE
```

24

```
MCRIB DRIP SCAM
ELISA IAGO CASA
SAFER WRAPPARTY
ANTENNAE TUNDRA
 OYL MAT ION
CUBANCIGARS
UNTIE EMT DOGS
STEM IOTAS AMAL
SONS SEA AMNIO
 CLUBHOPPING
MIA OAF ARE
INTERN FLAXSEED
SUBREDDIT ACUTE
TSAR EYRE MORAL
SETS REED STOLI
```

25

PINUP · ITCH · ALVA
ARENA · MATA · NYET
PARISTEXAS · GINS
AND · CIA · BRONTE
ATHENSGEORGIA
SELMA · TERESA
IDEAL · VINE · IKE
DARN · PREPS · GNAT
EMT · WHIR · PEALS
ARAFAT · ALLEY
NAPLESFLORIDA
ELAINE · TAR · TDS
VICE · TOLEDOOHIO
EVEN · WHAM · FREON
REDS · OOPS · FERRY

26

IRAN · DESI · ADAPT
NEMO · IRON · ROMEO
CHIC · GARBAGECAN
HAGUE · TOROS
BATTLEAXE · LIMB
SCAN · STALER
SOS · STAB · SPIRO
QUARTERBACKSACK
UNDER · YOGA · DYE
ACIDIC · EGAD
BEEB · ANKLEBOOT
IGLOO · AGNEW
YOUREFIRED · SITE
AANDM · SEER · ACRE
PRESS · YALE · TEAK

27

APPT · YAM · APLUS
FURY · MAKE · SEETO
TRIP · ALBA · KEANU
ESSENTIALWORKER
REMASTER · RUG
YES · GOTRICH
ASIGN · WIN · OSHA
HOMECOMINGQUEEN
AMMO · CUZ · UPEND
BEARHUG · MFA
GEL · MARIANAS
USMILITARYDRONE
STEAL · HIVE · MIND
DUNNO · EMIR · ERIE
AFUSS · MSN · DEER

28

JADA · MTWTF · LPS
EVIL · COWARD · ERA
NOSE · CMINOR · TIN
NICEJOB · STRAYED
ADO · LYRA · HUGOS
MAO · ASP · TOUTS
ORBS · HITECH · RFT
POOH · ADORE · OHSO
PCB · THERMO · WASP
SAUNA · RIA · ALI
FLINT · AFTS · RFK
LEAPDAY · RAKEDIN
ALT · EMOPOP · TOTO
OLE · MEDUSA · TWIT
SAD · RANTS · ANNS

29

HORA · ACID · CAMARO
OAHU · ROMA · REELED
GRUB · ISAY · ERRAND
BUDDYCOPMOVIES
CARE · FOES
BARNEYFIFE · OMIT
USB · TURN · PLANON
SUPS · BOTREE · DATA
KAILUA · ACAI · BAM
LEON · MAJORSCALE
NOAM · TADS
WHITEHOUSEDOGS
ROSARY · SOLE · EPIC
INLOVE · ELSA · ROKU
TEASES · DOER · STEP

30

CAST · ANON · PETAL
OTTO · LIPO · AGONY
REAR · POEM · COWER
GIMMEABREAK · EWE
INPEACE · MULL
NSA · PEPPERED
EMOTE · GOAL · GALA
RAN · ONCUE · CSI
INTL · HAUS · MAKES
EXHIBITS · LIL
EURO · GASLOGS
KGB · OUTOFPOCKET
YEARN · AXLE · ANNA
INLET · DEAL · POOL
VALVE · ANTS · SWAK

31

```
M O B   A S T R O S   E C H O
O U R   S T E A L S   M O O D
L S U   S P A C E N E E D L E
E T T U   A S K S   X R A Y S
    E N S U E     S T Y
E I F F E L T O W E R   A T E
S N O R E     S O C A L L E D
P U R E   E P C O T   A L P S
N I C E I D E A     E S T E E
U T E   F E R R I S W H E E L
    B O N     N E W E R
S N A I L   A C D C   D R A B
W O R L D S F A I R S   A X E
A L O E   P A R C E L   I L L
G A D S   F R A T T Y   N E T
```

32

```
P L A Y M A T E   A M B L E D
R U N O U T O N   M A R A C A
I N D U S T R Y   P R E Y O N
C A R D   E S A U   B E I N G
E R E   E S O   T O L D T O
    B L T   P O L E   O M G
B A H A I   M O P E   S N I T
A D A G E   A R I   A A M C O
L A S S   L P G A   D R E S S
I M A   E S P Y   C I A
    S T J U D E   A H N   S A M
S M A U G   D I D O   M O V E
T I S K E T   R I P T I D E S
A T T E N D   A E R A T O R S
T H E S E S   Q U A N T I T Y
```

33

```
S L E D S   O A S I S   P E T
A E S O P   W H I S T   R N A
G O L D E N E A G L E   I S M
    G L A D   M A N   C U E
F I R E U P   P A N C A K E D
A L A   N A V I   D I L L
T I T   K L I N E   L A Y L A
W A T T   M E A T S   S P U N
A D L I B   S T A I D   E N D
    E R O S   A L E E   A G E
B A S E H I T S   S P A R E S
A W N   E R E   S T E W
B A A   M E X I C A N F L A G
A R K   I N T R O   D U A N E
S E E   A S S E T   S L O A N
```

34

```
J A B   A P P L I E D   L P S
A M I   D U R A N T E   A L E
M A T C H B O X C A R   S A X
B R O O D       U S N A V Y
S O F A   S A A B   L E D S
    F L I N T M I C H I G A N
    S N O O P   L E G A T O
E T S   A R M   K I N   S E W
T R Y O N E   I N F R A
T I N D E R P R O F I L E
U P T O   R E B S   D R O P
    W A R B L E   L E O N E
F I X   F I R E S T A R T E R
E R E   F R E A K E D   I N K
Y E S   S E Q U I N S   C D S
```

35

```
A T W A R   R U G B Y   A S A
P H A S E   E M I L E   P C T
R I D I N G H A B I T   L A B
    N E S T L E   E P I T O M E
A M I   S O A K   U M P S
D I N G   B R E R R A B B I T
O N T A P   N O U N
    T O B E O R N O T T O B E
    A L O E   E V E N T
T R E B L E C L E F   A L T O
I A G O   S T O P   G R E
M I R A C L E   A R A B I A
E S E   P E B B L E B E A C H
L E T   A I O L I   L E N T O
Y D S   S A N T A   O N S E T
```

36

```
D O G   O A K     C H I E F
E R R   P I N A   A G E N D A
A C I D T R I P   W I I F I T
N A M E   S T E A M   S I T E
    R A P S   C A S T E
I N C I T E   R E N O   L C D
P O O D L E C U T   D R D R E
A D U E   D E N I M   A H A T
S E N D S   L O C A L D I V E
S S T   M A I N   L O I T E R
    Y O U I N   P A P A
P U S H   D E F E R   N U N S
S L E A Z E   T A K E T H A T
S T A R E S   C R E W   O N E
T A T E R   L Y E   H A M
```

37

```
ENDS  OCHO  MOBS
BARN  AHAB  AGUE
BREAKFAST ROLLS
 WIKI  THAI  ELSA
OHDEAR  TINT  DIP
BAE  STRANGELOOP
ILLS  EEG  SIGNS
  TBSP  ARTS
AWGEE  ALE  ACCT
THEWESTWING  AHA
TAT  ROWE  TACTIC
ATOI  LEEK  MALL
 INSIDEBASEBALL
 FILM  ZINE  ADIA
 STEP  ETTA  LYNX
```

38

```
SLIT  PETA  SKOSH
MACE  IRON  PALAU
ITEM  TEND  ATEST
THEPRICEISRIGHT
HES  EFT  USE
  SVU  STP  TEA
 TOTELLTHETRUTH
SONAR  ARR  AORTA
YOUBETYOURLIFE
RNS  ASP  OKS
  FAX  JAI  CTS
CLASSICGAMESHOW
OUSTS  HOPI  NINE
ONTOE  EBAN  ANYA
LEAPT  WING  PAST
```

39

```
VISA  PRIMP  AMOR
ESPN  LAMAR  ZONE
THEY  AGAME  APEX
 WHITECASTLE
 OTIS  SERE
ADJOIN  NEARBY
BAA  SURFACE  OUI
BING  MOORE  MSRP
AREAR  LOT  LIEGE
 YALE  EDS  URGE
SQUAD  PCT  BEARD
AUS  DELOUSE  RKO
META  LAUDE  ADIN
BEEP  SYRIA  TENN
ANNE  ASTOR  ANGE
```

40

```
AMID  CRAPO  IOWA
LAVA  RERUN  BRAG
ICEDCOFFEE  AGRA
  DOW  BETRAYS
EMMYS  PALAU  NOS
SOY  AIRPORTWIFI
PATH  NOR  TIC
 THEINSIDEINFO
  BRR  OED  GARB
EAUDEPARFUM  RCA
CDS  NOTIT  IMMAD
HOTBATH  SFO
ONEA  FEEFIFOFUM
EARN  UNLIT  DANA
DISK  LAMBS  YMCA
```

41

```
IMAC  SELLS  NOVA
BOCA  PLEAT  ARID
MANDARINORANGES
 TERRI  AMASS
 EGGWHITES
MEH  USHERIN  BOP
ERASE  ILK  DEERE
DISKS  LEI  SMEAR
ACHY  DENNY  OTTO
LAB  VISAGES  GET
 READ  SPAR
SPORCLE  PLACEBO
HEWN  ADORE  HEIR
URNS  PILOT  ONES
TEST  STEMS  OSLO
```

42

```
FIG  BRINE  LALA
IPA  FRIDAY  IZOD
JAZZERCISE  QUID
IDEAS  HOC  TURNS
  NSA  TAHOE
GAVE  DAIRYQUEEN
ODE  VIC  BURGLE
PIRATED  PRESALE
REDDER  TAI  DID
OUIJABOARD  USES
 ATSIX  SOS
SPECS  LCD  ADAPT
WOVE  SIOUXFALLS
AKIN  GEDDES  LIP
MELT  TRESS  YES
```

43

```
T I T L E   M E O W   I S L A
I S A A C   G A M E   P E A S
M O U T H O R G A N   A R T S
    C O N S E N T   V I E
G U S H E S   R I B J O I N T
A N T   S P F   Y U C C A S
S O A K   E A S T   D E E S
  K N U C K L E H E A D
P E A T   E Y R E   N O S H
P L A C I D   M L B   G N U
B A C K L A S H   P E R S O N
A T L   B L A M E M E
N E A T   B O D Y D O U B L E
D A I S   E M I T   A S T E R
J U M P   D O T H   N E W E R
```

44

```
F A N C Y   S I R I   P B J S
A R E A S   E P I C   E R I E
L I T T L E R O C K   L I V E
L A S S   R E D O   R O G E N
    G A I N   T U S H
  B L A C K A N D W H I T E S
B L A M E   O D O R   I T O
R A R E   J O R T S   A D H D
A I G   P A R T   O B E Y S
D R E S S R E H E A R S A L
    P A S S   S L O T
S T I L T   O N C E   R O L O
O R Z O   C O C O C H A N E L
B O Z O   C Z A R   A C T E D
S T A N   S E A T   S T O K E
```

45

```
A L O N G   C A S E   U P C S
L A B O R   H D T V   P L O W
P R I V A T E E Y E   T A R O
O D E   H A R P   F O Y E R
    P A Y I T F O R W A R D
S E S A M E   E L O N
O W E N   M A L A Y   A P E
H O T E L C A L I F O R N I A
O K S   A R N A Z   O N E S
    A C A I   M I S E R Y
H I D D E N C A M E R A
A D A M S   B O O K   T A P
L E V I   R O L L W I T H I T
L A I R   A X E L   N E R D S
E L S E   G O R Y   G L U E D
```

46

```
A W E S   T V P G   S L I C E
B A N E   H E A R   E A S E L
A T T N   E R I E   C D R O M
C U R D S A N D W H E Y
U S E   A L E   A D D S T O
S I E R R A   A I W E I W E I
    I A M B I C   A C L
  A N C H O R S A W E I G H
O D E   E L N I N O
Z I M B A B W E   I D C A R D
S N O O Z E   E M O   S E A
    G O Y O U R O W N W A Y
S O L A R   K N O T   A I R S
A W A R E   R I D E   P R E P
T E X T S   A X E S   A L D A
```

47

```
A D D U P   S C A M   S T E W
M A R T A   H E R A   T A M E
B R E A D   I N C H   E X I T
L I G H T E R T H A N A I R
E N S   H A T   T A D
    G A S   I R M A   C R Y
  H O L I E R T H A N T H O U
B E A U   I C E   H E L M
L A R G E R T H A N L I F E
Y D S   L A Z Y   E O N
    I L L   J A Y   L A Y
  I T S A L L R E L A T I V E
J A I L   I O U S   L O B E S
O G L E   E D I T   T O R R E
B O L T   D E N S   O K A Y S
```

48

```
S P U D   A G A V E   M E S H
O R S O   G O L A N   E C H O
B E E T R E P O R T   G O E R
S P R E E   E Y E B A L L S
    L A Z E   R E F I L E
R O L L R E V E R S A L
E W E   S T A R E   D O D G E
B L A H   A D O B O   P O E M
A S K O F   E D E N S   J A M
    M U S S E L M E M O R Y
S T R E E P   S E R A
P R E C L U D E   G R O P E
O A T H   M O U S S E C A L L
O D I E   E N R O N   O H O K
R E E F   S T O O L   S U P S
```